# the modern *cast iron cookbook*

# the modern cast iron cookbook

## A NEW GENERATION OF EASY, FRESH, AND HEALTHY RECIPES

**Tiffany La Forge**

Photography by Marija Vidal

**R**

ROCKRIDGE
PRESS

First Rockridge Press hardcover edition 2022

Originally published in trade paperback by Rockridge Press 2019

Rockridge Press and the Rockridge Press logo are trademarks or registered trademarks of Callisto Media Inc. and/or its affiliates in the United States and other countries and may not be used without written permission.

For general information on our other products and services, please contact our Customer Care Department within the United States at (866) 744-2665, or outside the United States at (510) 253-0500.

Hardcover ISBN: 979-8-88608-474-0 | Paperback ISBN: 978-1-64152-403-2
eBook ISBN: 978-1-64152-404-9

Manufactured in the United States of America

Interior and Cover Designer: Darren Samuel
Photo Art Director: Sue "Bees" Bischofberger
Editor: Clara Song Lee
Production Editor: Erum Khan

Photography © 2019 Marija Vidal.  Food styling by Cregg Green.
Author Photo courtesy of © KC England

10 9 8 7 6 5 4 3 2 1 0

*in loving memory of* **matthew bivone**

# contents

# introduction

*What comes to mind when you think of a cast iron pan? If you're like me, you might think of cast iron the way you think of an old friend—trusty, reliable, and secure. Maybe you feel that cast iron is outdated, too heavy, fickle, or difficult to maintain. Perhaps you've been thinking about buying one but are unsure where to start. Or maybe you don't think of it much at all and only dust it off to sear a steak once in a blue moon.*

*Whichever category you fall in, this book will help you think of cast iron in modern, innovative ways. Cast iron is the most versatile cookware there is, traveling from the campfire to the stove top to the oven to the center of the table. I hope these recipes inspire you to bring it along for new journeys.*

*Cast iron is classic, but it is not stale. Cast iron cookware has been a part of homes for hundreds of years for good reason. It's durable and inexpensive, and it can last lifetimes with a little care. No longer an antique shop relic, cast iron is staging a renaissance—proving its place in the present-day kitchen as we appreciate all it can do.*

*This heirloom cookware deserves a fresh new perspective. The following chapters contain recipes for everyone, including plant-based meals, easy weeknight dinners, and delicious showstoppers. We will roast vegetables to perfection, assemble savory casseroles, bake golden breads, and create inspired desserts. We'll explore international flavors, new techniques, and reinvented classics.*

*This is the modern cast iron.*

# chapter one
## A MODERN WAY TO COOK

*Passed down for generations and heavy with history, a cast iron pan is more of an investment than a purchase. As long as you treat it well, your cast iron cookware will last more than a lifetime. This chapter answers all of your cast iron questions and concerns—from which to buy to how to clean to seasoning—step by step.*

# WHY CAST IRON COOKING TODAY?

While there are so many benefits to cast iron, here are my favorites:

**Versatility.** I believe cast iron is the most versatile cookware you will ever own. It does many things and does them well. Cast iron skillets produce crispy fried chicken, tender roasted vegetables, and perfectly seared meats. Dutch ovens develop deep, savory flavors ideal for braising, stews, and sauces. And all cast iron goes from the stove top to the oven with ease. You can even bring your cast iron outdoors and cook cornbread, beans, and one-pot dishes right over the campfire. You can't say that about your other kitchen cookware.

**Health.** Many love the convenience and low maintenance of nonstick pans but don't think about the negative health effects. Cast iron can be considered the original "green" pan, as it provides a natural nonstick coating from the polymerization of oil (more on that in the Seasoning Science section, page 6). Unlike some nonstick cookware, such as Teflon, cast iron does not release or produce toxic fumes. Cast iron can also give your iron levels a boost, as a small amount of iron releases into food during cooking.

**Staying Power.** Unlike other cookware, you'll probably never have to replace your cast iron pan. Cast iron is nearly impossible to ruin and can be passed down for generations. Pans made in the 1800s are still being used today—getting even better with time and aging beautifully. Now that's what I call sustainability.

# CAST IRON MYTHS

There has been some controversy over cast iron. Let's debunk the eight most common myths.

### Myth #1: Never use soap to wash your cast iron pan.

Truth: You can use a minimal amount of soap to clean your cast iron as needed without it affecting your pan's seasoning. Yes, soap removes oil, but the oil used to season a cast iron skillet is polymerized and bonded with the metal.

### Myth #2: Cast iron cookware heats evenly.

Truth: While cast iron pans are excellent at maintaining heat, they're pretty poor at conducting it. This is why preheating your cast iron pan is so important. Before cooking anything in cast iron, preheat the pan for at least 10 minutes on the stove over medium heat, rotating often.

## STAGING A COMEBACK

Cast iron has been around for centuries. The oldest cast iron pieces on record date back to the fifth century BC and are from China, where iron was used to make pots, pagodas, and plowshares.

However, the acclaim of globalizing cast iron cookware is credited to British ironmaster Abraham Darby. In the early 1700s, Darby developed and patented a method for creating cast iron cookware that was thinner, cheaper to make, and could be mass-produced in larger quantities.

Cast iron was used often because of its amazing ability to withstand large amounts of heat for long periods of time, which made it ideal for cooking over campfires, fireplaces, and hearths. From the pioneers to the wealthy to the members of the Lewis and Clark Expedition, everyone used cast iron cookware.

The late 1800s saw the rise of many cast iron cookware manufacturers, including Giswold, Wagner Ware, and the only one still around today, Lodge Manufacturing. Cast iron cookware remained a kitchen staple until its popularity declined in the twentieth century with the rise of aluminum, stainless steel, and coated nonstick options.

But this vintage pan has staged a successful comeback, as cast iron cookware has once again become prominent in the modern kitchens of chefs and home cooks alike. Professional chefs swear by their skillets, while colorful, high-end enameled cast iron appears on countless wedding registries across the globe. Cast iron is a worthy investment—for your health, your home, and your culinary ventures.

**Myth #3: You can't use metal cooking utensils in your cast iron.**

Truth: Metal spatulas, tongs, and spoons won't ruin or chip your pan's seasoning. The seasoning isn't just a "coating"—it is bonded to the pan and more resilient than you think.

**Myth #4: You can't cook acidic foods in cast iron.**

Truth: You can cook with tomatoes and wine in your cast iron in moderate amounts (in fact, several of the recipes in this book include those ingredients!). As long as your cast iron is well-seasoned, cooking with acidic foods isn't an issue. However, it's best not to cook acidic foods in cast iron for a long period of time (like slow-simmered tomato sauce, for example).

**Myth #5: You can only use cast iron cookware on gas stoves, not electric.**

Truth: Cast iron is great for just about any form of cooking, including electric stoves. However, it may take slightly longer to cook on electric versus gas stoves when using cast iron, and preheating is especially crucial. Additionally, to avoid scratching, be sure to never slide a cast iron pan on a glass-top stove.

**Myth #6: You don't have to season a pre-seasoned skillet.**

Truth: While you could use a pre-seasoned skillet as soon as you get home from the store, it's always a good idea to season the pan yourself. This will provide an additional layer of protection and get you accustomed to the process, too. And remember: the more you use your pan, the better it will get.

**Myth #7: Rust on a cast iron means it's ruined.**

Truth: Even if your pan is rusted, it's not ruined. Unless a cast iron's structure is compromised (cracked or rusted through), it's salvageable. There's almost nothing a little elbow grease and a good YouTube tutorial video can't fix when it comes to cast iron.

**Myth #8: Cast iron cookware is fragile and/or difficult to maintain.**

Truth: Cast iron is tough as nails and very, very difficult to completely ruin. With proper (and easy) maintenance, your cast iron will last you a lifetime!

# CHOOSING A CAST IRON PAN

There are many different ways to acquire your first cast iron pan—whether it is passed down to you from your grandmother or you purchase it on sale at Target. Neither way is wrong, but here are some things to consider when it comes to choosing a cast iron pan to suit your needs and budget.

## CAST IRON BASICS

When choosing the perfect cast iron pan for you, think about what you plan on using it for most. A large (12- to 14-plus-inch) pan is ideal for searing steaks and making hearty one-pot meals, while a trusty 10-inch skillet is more compact and easier to handle. As a starter pan, I recommend a pre-seasoned Lodge, which can easily be found for around $20 (more on different brands on page 7). Additionally, don't be afraid to shop for cast iron pans at thrift shops, garage sales, and antique stores. Look for pans that are in good condition and free from warping, pitting, and cracks.

## WEIGHT

Cast iron pans are heavy; there's no denying that. The 12-inch skillet I use on a daily basis weighs in at about 7 pounds. A cast iron's heft is also what makes it so great for cooking food evenly and maintaining heat. If you need a more portable option, there are many different lightweight cast iron pans on the market. These pans are crafted in metal molds and typically have steel handles that are attached to the skillet separately. They are designed to be thinner, take less time to heat, and, of course, weigh much less.

Lightweight pans can make a good starter option for getting accustomed to using cast iron. But, in my opinion, nothing will beat the traditional cast iron skillet. Lightweight cast iron can heat unevenly, and, while it takes less time to warm up, it also maintains heat less effectively. Lastly, these pans are known to be less durable than their traditional counterparts. If you're looking for quality cast iron that's lighter and thinner, check out the modern artisan brands I recommend on page 8.

## SHAPES AND SIZES

Cast iron comes in an array of shapes, sizes, and colors. Let's explore some of the most popular types and sizes, many of which are featured in this book.

**Skillets.** Cast iron skillets are commonly available in mini (3.5-inch), small (8-inch), medium (10-inch), and large (12- to 17-inch) sizes. Mini skillets are great for single fried eggs and individual desserts. Small skillets are good for hot dips or small sides, and medium skillets work for quick breads, baked oatmeal, oven-puffed pancakes, and camping. The 12-inch skillet is the one I use and recommend most, but you might need an even larger pan if you're feeding a family. Large skillets are excellent choices for searing meats and making casseroles and one-pot meals.

**Dutch Ovens.** The Dutch oven may also be referred to as a French oven, cocotte, or camping oven. They typically come in oval, round, or novelty (e.g., heart-shaped) options that range from 4 to 10 quarts in size. Dutch ovens are perfect for soups, stews, chilis, beans, braising meats, and pasta dishes.

**Grill Pans and Griddles.** A cast iron grill pan can be round or square and can range from 6 to 12 inches in size. These pans are excellent for making grilled meats, fruits, fish, and vegetables. Griddles come in large rectangular options that are meant to be used on your stove top and work well for making pancakes, burgers, or breakfast for a crowd. There are several cast iron options on the market that offer a reversible 2-in-1 griddle/grill pan.

**Specialty Pans.** Novelty cast iron pans are available in various shapes and sizes, from the aebleskiver pan to the playful cornstick pan. If you're looking to make something specific, there's probably a cast iron pan for it. Examples include scone/wedge pans, muffin pans, crêpe pans, drop biscuit pans, woks, and melting/fondue pots.

## ENAMELED PANS

Enameled cast iron pans come in dozens of colorful options and require less maintenance than traditional cast iron because they don't need to be seasoned and are easier to clean. Enameled cast iron is nonreactive and can cook acidic foods for a longer period of time, which makes it a better choice for things like slow-simmered tomato sauce and wine-braised meats.

While enameled pans are also oven-safe (typically up to 500°F), they shouldn't be used on the grill or open campfire. Additionally, enameled pans are not as good at charring meats as bare cast iron. They're also easier to chip, can stain easily, and are typically more expensive.

# SEASONING SCIENCE

Many people are intimidated by the word *seasoning* when it comes to cast iron, but it's not as difficult as you think. Seasoning this cookware properly—and maintaining that seasoning—is vital to successful, delicious, nonstick cast iron cooking.

## WHAT IS SEASONING?

If you've been blessed with a family heirloom, you may not realize how much work and patience went into getting that skillet perfectly seasoned. Even with pre-seasoned cast iron cookware, you will need to re-season the pan eventually (and I actually recommend doing so as soon as you get a new pan, even if it's a hand-me-down).

The process of seasoning is not as scary as it sounds. It basically involves oiling and heating the pan to make it nonstick and to prevent it from rusting. Over time, this seasoning will create the natural slick patina every cast iron strives for.

## TOP BRANDS

With so many cast iron cookware contenders on the market, it can be hard to know which brand to choose and why. Here are some of my favorite brands, leading in quality and features.

### CLASSIC CAST IRON

**LODGE.** As one of the oldest cast iron manufacturing companies still in business today, Lodge has survived two world wars and the Great Depression. Lodge produces high-quality, affordable, American-made cast iron pans that I am proud to use in my own kitchen. From colorful enameled skillets to specialty pans to camping ovens, Lodge offers a vast variety of cast iron cookware. You can easily find this brand at mass retailers or on Amazon, and their pre-seasoned skillets make excellent and affordable starter options.

**VICTORIA.** Victoria has been making cast iron cookware since 1939. They specialize in sturdy, high-quality, traditional cast iron pans. Victoria offers skillets, Dutch ovens, grill pans, woks, and more. Like Lodge, Victoria is very affordable and comes pre-seasoned.

### ENAMELED SKILLETS AND DUTCH OVENS

**LE CREUSET.** Le Creuset is considered the crème de la crème of cast iron, and I don't know a single foodie who doesn't swoon over it. Although expensive, Le Creuset specializes in high quality and strict standards that ensure your cast iron lasts a lifetime. Their cookware comes in over two dozen stunning colors and limited editions, from sugary pastels and vivid brights to ombre hues.

**STAUB.** Staub offers a variety of cast iron cookware and bakeware but is known best for their French ovens and colorful cocottes. This French company is favored by professional chefs and offers an excellent lifetime warranty program. Like Le Creuset, Staub is pricey, but not impossible to find on sale.

### ARTISAN

There are many new, modern cast iron manufacturers on the market who are creating artisan and handcrafted cookware that resembles the polished vintage pans of the past. These cast iron options are made in America and start at about $150 for a medium skillet. Artisan cast iron brands include Smithey Ironware, popular for their satin-smooth finish; FINEX, which features their patented and unique octagon shape; and Butter Pat Industries and Field Company, which both promise lighter and smoother cast iron alternatives that don't sacrifice quality.

## THE SCIENCE BEHIND SEASONING

A natural nonstick patina is the result of a well-seasoned cast iron pan. This patina is achieved by coating your pan in thin layers of oil and heating it, which causes polymerization. This process causes the fat chains in the oil to cross-link together and become bonded to the metal, forming a protective and resilient plastic-like coating that keeps your cast iron rust-free and nonstick.

Additionally, the fat you use to cook with and to wipe down your pan after cleaning will help protect and improve your seasoning. Your cast iron will only get better the more you use it.

## IS YOUR PAN WELL-SEASONED?

A properly seasoned cast iron pan will look sleek, slightly shiny, and dark black and should not be sticky (this is the result of too much oil). The seasoning should not flake off in large pieces, and the pan should be nonstick. Building that beautiful patina and seasoning takes time, so use your cast iron as often as possible. Bonus points for frying chicken and cooking bacon!

## SEASONING YOUR SKILLET

Most cast iron cookware today is sold pre-seasoned, so all you need to do is give it a quick cleaning before cooking. (However, it's always a good idea to season it again, if possible.) But maybe you purchased unseasoned cookware, or it's time to re-season your own skillet or that older thrift market find. Here's how to do it in five simple steps:

**Step 1: Clean your cast iron pan well using soap and warm water.** (Head to page 12 for cast iron cleaning tips and tools.) If your pan has rust, use a steel wool brush to remove it.

**Step 2: Dry the pan thoroughly with a kitchen towel.**

**Step 3: Coat the entire surface of the pan (interior and exterior) with a thin layer of edible oil that's been thoroughly and evenly rubbed in.** Any oil will do the trick, but I recommend vegetable, flaxseed, coconut, or canola oil.

**Step 4: Place the oiled pan in a cold oven upside down with foil below it to catch any drippings.** Turn the oven to 400°F. When it reaches temperature, bake the pan for 1 hour. At the 1-hour mark, turn the oven off and let the pan cool in the oven.

**Step 5: Repeat this process, if desired, up to three or four times to really develop a resilient seasoning, although it's not mandatory.**

### HOW TO TELL WHEN YOUR CAST IRON NEEDS TO BE RE-SEASONED

One of the first and most important indicators that your cast iron is due for a re-seasoning is when your food begins to stick. Additionally, if the cooking surface of the pan begins to turn grayish, becomes sticky, or looks dull, it's definitely time to re-season. On rare occasions, rust may build up on a pan or food might taste metallic, at which point the pan will need to be thoroughly cleaned and all rust removed before re-seasoning.

# CAST IRON TECHNIQUES

Let's explore the best cooking techniques for cast iron cookware—and which to avoid.

**Roasting and Braising.** Cast iron is the ideal vessel for roasting and braising. Proteins can achieve the perfect sear before traveling to the oven to finish cooking. Use cast iron to make roasted chicken, pot roast, braised short ribs, and oven-roasted vegetables.

**Searing.** There's a reason the cast iron skillet is a favorite for searing steaks. Its high heat allows meats to get a caramelized, flavorful crust while still remaining juicy in the center.

**Blackening.** Blackened meats and fish, popular in Cajun cuisine, turn out best when cooked in a hot cast iron skillet.

**Frying.** The benefits of frying in your cast iron are twofold: you'll get perfectly golden chicken, zucchini (page 84), or cauliflower (page 66), and your pan will get an extra layer of seasoning.

**Stir-Fries.** Cast iron is a great choice for stir-fries and fried rice. Since cast iron holds heat so well, it can act similarly to a wok. I love using my skillet for Hawaiian Breakfast Fried Rice (page 28) to get those crispy little bits (the best part).

**Baking.** A favorite for cornbreads, crisps, cobblers, and even cake, your cast iron skillet can be used as you would use a pie pan or baking dish.

**Campfire Cooking.** You can take your cast iron from the kitchen to the outdoors without a hitch. Cast iron is perfect for cooking just about anything over open flame, from one-pot skillet meals to Campfire S'mores Banana Boats (page 158).

However, there are a few things cast iron isn't the best choice for. This includes cooking delicate fish, preparing highly acidic foods for long periods of time, and boiling water. It's also best to avoid sticky foods (like eggs, pancakes, and rice) until your pan is well-seasoned.

Lastly, be aware that cooking in cast iron may cause some foods to take on previous flavors. Be mindful of this when cooking savory meals and desserts in the same skillet. I like to have a dedicated skillet just for breads and sweets.

## CAST IRON COOKING SUCCESS

Follow these simple tips and tricks for successful cast iron cooking.

**Preheat Your Pan.** Always preheat your cast iron pan on the stove for at least 10 minutes. Cast iron takes longer to warm up than other cookware, and a piping hot pan is essential to nonstick cooking. But you don't need very high heat—medium heat works fine for cooking just about anything in cast iron.

**Safety First.** Always use two hands when holding or transporting a heavy cast iron pan, and remember: Cast iron gets **hot.** Use pot holders, oven mitts, or a handle cover to touch cast iron, even when cooking on the stove top. When presenting cast iron dishes at the table, use a trivet and keep a towel on the handle to signify that it's still hot.

**Keep It Dry.** Make sure your pan is always thoroughly dried, and never let it air-dry. Dry it immediately after cleaning with a kitchen towel or in a hot oven. Even the smallest amount of water will cause rust.

**Oil After Each Use.** After cleaning your cast iron and while it's still warm, rub the dry pan with a teaspoon of oil and let it absorb before putting it away.

**Store Properly.** Never store food in a cast iron pan. Always remove leftovers and store them separately. You can store your cast iron pans stacked, but keep a layer of paper towels or a kitchen towel between them. This helps prevent rust from any residual moisture lingering on the bottom of the pans.

**Use It!** This may seem redundant, but the best tip for cast iron cooking is to use your pan often. I can't stress enough that the more you use your cast iron pan, the better it will get. With frequent use, that sleek black patina will soon be yours.

## COOKING TOOLS

Having the right tools and equipment makes a world of difference in the kitchen. Here are my favorites when it comes to the recipes in this book, organized into essential and optional categories:

### NEED-TO-HAVES

**The Basics.** A well-equipped kitchen should have all of the basics, including a cutting board, a sharp knife, a trusty wooden spoon, spatulas (both a turner for flipping and a rubber or silicone one for baking), a whisk, oven mitts, kitchen towels, a can opener, and a vegetable peeler.

**Tongs.** Tongs are very handy in cast iron cooking when it comes to searing meats, frying, and turning steaks.

**Set of Mixing/Prep Bowls.** Most of the recipes in this book are one-pot, but a good set of prep bowls in varying sizes is needed.

**Grater.** You'll need a grater to grate cheese, shred potatoes for latkes, and grate zucchini for bread.

**Zester.** A Microplane works wonders for zesting citrus and grating fresh spices like nutmeg, and it's my go-to for grating ginger and garlic.

**Measuring Spoons and Cups.** A complete set of measuring spoons and measuring cups—both liquid and dry—is necessary for the recipes in this book, especially in baking.

**Handheld or Standing Mixer.** You'll need a handheld electric mixer (or standing electric mixer, if you have one) for the dessert and bread recipes in this book.

**Trivet.** You'll want a trivet if you plan to serve recipes in hot cast iron cookware at the table.

### NICE-TO-HAVES

**Thermometer.** A thermometer is helpful if you plan to do a lot of frying in your cast iron or want to check the internal temperature of meats.

**Mandoline.** A mandoline will get even, thin slices of potato for gratins or chips prepped in no time.

**Oil Splatter Screen.** This will help keep oil off your walls—and yourself—when frying.

**Universal Lid.** A universal lid is handy to have around, as most cast iron skillets do not come with lids.

**Hot Handle Holder.** A silicone or heat-proof handle holder protects from red-hot cast iron handles, but towels or mitts work just fine, too.

**Grill Press.** A small cast iron grill press is great for burgers or pressed sandwiches, but a smaller skillet can work just as well.

**Pastry Cutter.** A pastry cutter is really helpful for cutting butter into flour for pie crusts, biscuits, and streusel, but a hefty fork will work in a pinch.

## CLEANING YOUR CAST IRON

When it comes to cleaning your cast iron, you've got options. Here are some of the best methods, tools, and tricks—including both what you should and should never do.

### ALWAYS

- Clean as soon as possible, and when the pan is still warm. Avoid letting food sit in it for too long.
- Use hot water.
- Dry it immediately.

## NEVER

- Put it in the dishwasher.

- Let it soak in water.

- Use abrasive cleaning tools like steel wool and metal scouring pads (unless you're trying to remove rust and plan on re-seasoning).

## CLEANING YOUR CAST IRON IN THREE EASY STEPS

**Step 1:** *Rinse the pan with hot water, and use a nonabrasive sponge or brush to clean.* *Use a small amount of soap, if needed.*

**Step 2:** *Dry the pan immediately with a lint-free kitchen towel or paper towels.* *Never let the pan air-dry.*

**Step 3:** *Once dry and while still warm, pour a teaspoon of oil into the skillet and rub it into the entire interior surface.*

## CAST IRON CLEANING TOOLS

**Chainmail Scrubber.** Chainmail scrubbers are great choices for cleaning cast iron. These scrubbers are made from smooth stainless steel rings that remove stuck-on food without harming your pan's surface or seasoning. You can find these easily on Amazon.

**Brush.** You can find a variety of cast iron cleaning brushes, especially from cast iron manufacturers like Lodge. Stiff-bristled nylon brushes are good choices.

**Scraper.** A good, durable polycarbonate pan scraper with rounded edges will make cleaning your cast iron much, much easier.

## EXTRA-DIRTY SKILLETS

If your pan has stubborn stuck-on food, follow these two tricks. First, use some kosher salt mixed with a splash of water to form a paste to scrub the pan with. This mildly abrasive paste is great for those hard-to-remove bits. If that doesn't work, boil a small amount of water in your cast iron on the stove top, which will loosen and release food residue.

# MAKE THE MOST OF YOUR CAST IRON

These are some of my favorite ways to use my cast iron, from the everyday to the unexpected.

**Pizza.** No pizza pan? No problem. Cast iron skillets are terrific for baking pizzas, focaccia, and flatbreads.

**Breads.** A golden skillet cornbread (page 42) is one of the most popular uses for cast iron, but your pan can also cook naan (page 44), biscuits (page 52), and zucchini bread (page 57).

**Pressed Sandwiches.** These are some of my favorite things to prepare in cast iron, thanks to that extra-crispy crust. To make a great pressed sandwich, use a larger cast iron skillet for cooking and a smaller one for placing on top to press.

**Casseroles and One-Pot Meals.** Chicken pot pie (page 116), shepherd's pie (pages 96 and 152), vegetarian casseroles, and gratins galore—you'll find them all in this book.

**Baked Egg Dishes.** From Spring Green Shakshuka (page 31) to Eggs in Purgatory (page 35) to your classic frittata, brunch is a breeze with a cast iron skillet that goes from the stove top to the oven with ease.

**Pancakes.** A trusty 10-inch skillet will make the most glorious Dutch baby (page 27), while a cast iron griddle gives new life to Sunday morning pancakes.

**Pies and Cobblers.** Cast iron skillets can double as baking dishes and pie pans to make delicious desserts like tarte tatin (page 156), skillet cookies, cobblers, and crumbles.

**Oven-to-Table.** We know that the faithful cast iron can go from the stove top to the oven effortlessly, but my favorite part is that it also makes for a gorgeous presentation when served at the table. Cook, bake, and present attractive dishes like Rosemary-Parsnip Pommes Anna with Goat Cheese (page 62) and Provençal Heirloom Tomatoes (page 69) all in your skillet. Bonus: Cast iron keeps food hotter for longer, too!

# WASTE NOT

Follow these easy tips to help reduce food waste in your kitchen:

**Store Smart.** Food often gets wasted because it wasn't stored properly and went stale or spoiled. When opening a box of something like cereal or crackers, place it in an airtight container instead of keeping it in the opened box. Also, be mindful of the best place to store specific foods (refrigerator, freezer, or room temperature) and which foods shouldn't be stored together.

**Freeze.** Don't be afraid to use your freezer. Save leftover herbs by chopping them, placing them in ice cube trays, filling with olive oil, and freezing. Slice too-ripe bananas or other fruits and freeze them in zip-top plastic bags for smoothies. Freeze leftover wine or broth/stock in ice cube trays.

**Grate Blocks of Cheese.** When grating cheese for a recipe, grate the whole block at once and keep the rest sealed in the refrigerator. You can then quickly add shredded cheese to salads, scrambles, or quesadillas.

**Use Stale Bread.** If bread has sat on the counter too long (or no one wants to eat the end pieces), process it into fresh bread crumbs for gratins or make croutons or Savory Breakfast Bread Pudding (page 30).

**Make Your Own Stock.** Save vegetable trimmings like carrot peelings, leek and fennel tops, onion ends, and celery leaves for making your own broths and stocks. Keep a bag in the freezer, and add your scraps until you have enough for a batch of stock.

**Pickle It.** Consider pickling any vegetables you don't plan on using anytime soon.

**Reinvent Leftovers.** If no one is excited for leftovers the next day, use them to create something entirely new. Leftover rice makes excellent fried rice, roasted vegetables are great for pizzas or frittatas, and stews or meats can be transformed into completely different meals like shepherd's pie (pages 96 and 152), enchiladas, pasta dishes, and casseroles.

# SHOP SMART

Follow these easy tips to help save money, save time, and reduce food waste:

**Shop the Bulk Bins.** Items like nuts, grains, beans, specialty flours, dried fruits, and more are often less expensive in bulk bins, and you can buy the exact amount you need.

**Know When to Buy Big.** Buying in bulk might still be a smart choice, even if you don't have a large family, but focus on nonperishable, frozen, and canned items.

**Buy Smarter.** Sometimes buying only what you need is the best way to minimize food waste. To do this, get meat from the butcher's counter instead of buying it packaged, so you can ask for exact quantities/weight. The same goes for the deli and fish counters.

**Meal Plan.** Having a meal plan and sticking to it can save you both money and time.

**Shop More Often.** One big grocery haul a week may result in more food waste than planned. Shopping more frequently for lower quantities can help.

**Go Off-Brand.** Many supermarkets sell their own items, which are often less expensive (and can even contain better ingredients) than their popular brand-name counterparts.

**Buy Local and In Season.** Fresh produce in season not only tastes better, but it also costs less. Buying local from farmers' markets or co-ops is also a great way to support your community.

**Clip Coupons.** Don't be afraid to use coupons! Smartphone apps like Ibotta and websites such as Coupons.com now make this easier than ever.

# MAKING THESE RECIPES

You'll find the following labels on the recipes throughout this book to help you manage your time and adhere to any dietary needs:

## Preferences

- **5-Ingredient:** recipes that use 5 ingredients or fewer (not counting salt, pepper, or cooking fat)
- **One Pan:** recipes that require only one cast iron pan to cook an entire meal
- **Quick & Easy:** recipes that take 30 minutes or less to prepare from start to finish
- **Weekday/Weeknight:** recipes that take an hour or less to prepare from start to finish

## Dietary Requirements

- **Gluten-Free**
- **Grain-Free**
- **Vegan**
- **Vegetarian**

*Spring Green Shakshuka*
*page 31*

# chapter two
# BREAKFAST & BRUNCH

# ROOT VEGETABLE AND BACON HASH

**12″ SKILLET** / Gluten-Free / Grain-Free / One Pan / Weekday

**Serves 6 / Prep time: 10 minutes / Cook time: 40 minutes**

I love root vegetables so much that I named my blog after one. Using both regular and sweet potatoes makes for an interesting breakfast hash, both in flavor and texture. When complementary parsnip, carrot, leek, and applewood-smoked bacon are added to the mix, magic happens.

6 thick-cut applewood-smoked bacon slices, diced

1 leek, white and light green part only, halved lengthwise and thinly sliced

4 gold potatoes, peeled and diced

1 sweet potato, peeled and diced

1 parsnip, peeled and diced

1 carrot, peeled and diced

Salt

Freshly ground black pepper

2 garlic cloves, minced

1 tablespoon chopped fresh sage

1 teaspoon chopped fresh rosemary

6 large eggs

1. Preheat the oven to 425°F. Preheat the skillet over medium heat. Put the bacon in the hot pan and cook until crisp and evenly browned, about 8 minutes. Transfer the bacon to a paper towel–lined plate, reserving 2 tablespoons of bacon fat in the skillet.

2. Add the leek and cook until softened but not browned, about 3 minutes. Add the gold potato, sweet potato, parsnip, and carrot. Stir to coat the vegetables in the bacon fat, and season with salt and pepper. Cook until tender, golden brown, and caramelized, 15 to 20 minutes.

3. Add the garlic, sage, and rosemary. Cook until fragrant and the garlic is softened, about 2 minutes. Stir the cooked bacon back in.

4. Use a spoon to make 6 small divots in the hash, and crack an egg into each. Top the eggs with salt and pepper. Transfer to the oven and bake until the egg whites are set and the eggs are cooked to your liking, 8 to 10 minutes.

5. Serve hot.

**SUBSTITUTION TIP:** Make this vegan by leaving out the bacon and eggs. Just use 2 tablespoons of cooking oil in place of the bacon fat when cooking, and top with a spoonful of apple butter.

# ITALIAN GREEN EGGS AND HAM FRITTATA

**10" SKILLET** / Gluten-Free / Grain-Free / One Pan / Weekday

**Serves 8 / Prep time: 10 minutes / Cook time: 35 minutes**

I loved Dr. Seuss's *Green Eggs and Ham* growing up and thought, "I would absolutely eat that, Sam-I-Am!" This recipe is an ode to that whimsical imaginary recipe. Or, at least, my version of it—with an Italian spin. Tuscan kale, Italian ham (pancetta), and fontina and Parmesan cheeses combine to form this easy, savory frittata.

2 tablespoons extra-virgin olive oil, divided

4 ounces pancetta, diced

1 yellow onion, diced

1 green bell pepper, diced

Salt

Freshly ground black pepper

2 garlic cloves, minced

3 cups chopped Tuscan kale

8 large eggs

½ cup whole milk

½ teaspoon dried thyme

¼ teaspoon dried oregano

¾ cup grated fontina cheese

½ cup grated Parmesan cheese

Chopped fresh parsley, for serving (optional)

1. Preheat the oven to 400°F, and preheat the skillet over medium heat. Heat 1 tablespoon of olive oil in the skillet, add the pancetta, and cook until crisp and browned, about 5 minutes.

2. Transfer the pancetta to a paper towel–lined plate and set aside. Add the remaining tablespoon of olive oil to the skillet, and swirl to coat the sides and surface. Add the onion and bell pepper. Cook until softened, about 6 minutes, and season with salt and pepper. Stir in the garlic and kale and cook for a few minutes, until the kale is wilted and tender. Stir back in the pancetta.

3. In a medium bowl, whisk the eggs with the milk, thyme, oregano, and fontina cheese. Season with salt and pepper. Pour the egg mixture over the vegetables. Sprinkle with the Parmesan cheese, and transfer to the oven.

4. Bake the frittata until set, about 20 minutes. Serve topped with chopped fresh parsley (if using).

**INGREDIENT TIP:** Pancetta is commonly found pre-diced in the deli section of most grocers.

# CHICKEN SAUSAGE, GOAT CHEESE, AND BROCCOLINI FRITTATA

**12" SKILLET** / **Gluten-Free** / **Grain-Free** / **One Pan** / **Weekday**

Serves 8 / Prep time: 10 minutes / Cook time: 35 minutes

Chicken sausage is not just for dinner. Here, Italian chicken sausage combines with sweet, earthy broccolini and red bell pepper. Chicken sausage is lower in fat and calories than pork sausage but still big in flavor. I crave this frittata for both breakfast and supper.

2 tablespoons extra-virgin olive oil

½ onion, diced

6 ounces fully cooked Italian chicken sausage, diced

2 garlic cloves, minced

1 red bell pepper, diced

2 cups chopped broccolini

Salt

Freshly ground black pepper

8 large eggs

½ cup whole milk

¼ cup grated Parmesan cheese

4 ounces goat cheese, crumbled

¼ cup chopped fresh parsley

1. Preheat the oven to 400°F, and preheat the skillet over medium heat. Heat the olive oil in the pan, and swirl to coat the surface and sides. Add the onion and cook until softened and translucent, about 5 minutes.

2. Add the sausage and cook until lightly browned, about 5 minutes.

3. Stir in the garlic, bell pepper, and broccolini. Season with salt and pepper and cook until the vegetables are crisp-tender, about 5 minutes.

4. In a large bowl, whisk the eggs with the milk, Parmesan cheese, and generous pinches of salt and pepper. Sprinkle the vegetable mixture evenly with the crumbled goat cheese, and pour the eggs over top.

5. Transfer to the oven and bake until the eggs are set and the goat cheese is slightly browned, 15 to 18 minutes.

6. Top with the parsley, season with pepper, and serve.

**INGREDIENT TIP:** Although most think broccolini is just baby broccoli, it's actually a hybrid vegetable of broccoli and Chinese kale (gai lan). You can use broccoli instead, if you prefer.

# MIGAS WITH SOY CHORIZO

**12″ SKILLET** / Gluten-Free / One Pan / Vegetarian / Weekday

**Serves 6 / Prep time: 10 minutes / Cook time: 25 minutes**

I've been making my migas with soy chorizo for years, and even my meat-loving friends enjoy them. Soy chorizo imparts a savory, spicy flavor, but if you aren't ready to give it a try, you could use chorizo here instead or leave it out altogether.

2 tablespoons extra-virgin olive oil, divided

1 tablespoon unsalted butter

6 (6-inch) corn tortillas, halved and cut into short strips

Salt

1 yellow onion, diced

1 green bell pepper, diced

1 red bell pepper, diced

1 jalapeño pepper, diced

3 garlic cloves, minced

8 ounces soy chorizo

8 large eggs

¼ cup whole milk

½ teaspoon ground cumin

Freshly ground black pepper

2 plum tomatoes, seeded and diced

½ cup shredded pepper Jack cheese

⅓ cup crumbled Cotija cheese

⅓ cup chopped fresh cilantro

Lime wedges, thinly sliced radish, and avocado, for serving (optional)

1. Preheat the skillet over medium heat. Heat 1 tablespoon of olive oil and the butter in the pan. Add the tortilla strips and cook until golden, about 3 minutes. Transfer to a paper towel–lined plate, and season with salt.

2. Add the remaining tablespoon of oil to the pan, along with the onion. Cook until softened and translucent, about 5 minutes, then add the bell peppers, jalapeño pepper, and garlic. Cook until the vegetables are tender, about 5 minutes.

3. Add the soy chorizo, break it up with a wooden spoon, and cook until browned, 5 to 7 minutes.

4. In a large bowl, whisk the eggs with the milk and cumin, and season with salt and pepper. Add the eggs to the pan and gently stir until scrambled, 3 to 5 minutes. Add the fried tortillas, diced tomato, and pepper Jack cheese. Gently fold until everything is incorporated.

5. Top the skillet with the Cotija cheese and cilantro. Serve with lime wedges, radish, and avocado, if desired.

# MAPLE-MIXED BERRY BAKED OATMEAL

**10" SKILLET** / Gluten-Free / One Pan / Vegetarian / Weekday

**Serves 6 / Prep time: 5 minutes / Cook time: 55 minutes**

To be honest, I have never really been a fan of oatmeal. I don't care for the texture, and if I eat it at all, it needs to be warm (no cold overnight oats for this lady). But when I was introduced to the magic that is baked oatmeal, my stance on oatmeal changed. The skillet is great for toasting the oats beforehand to give them a nuttier flavor. Feel free to experiment here and use any fruit that's currently in season.

1½ cups rolled oats

½ teaspoon salt

1 teaspoon baking powder

½ teaspoon ground cinnamon

¼ teaspoon ground nutmeg

⅓ cup sliced or chopped almonds

1¾ cups whole milk

1 large egg

1 teaspoon vanilla extract

⅓ cup maple syrup, plus more
   for serving

2 tablespoons unsalted butter

2 cups fresh mixed berries (raspberries,
   blueberries, and chopped
   strawberries), plus more for serving

2 tablespoons brown sugar

Warm whole milk (optional)

1. Preheat the oven to 350°F, and preheat the skillet over medium heat. Add the oats to the dry, hot skillet and cook for 3 minutes, until fragrant and slightly toasted. Transfer to a large bowl.

2. Add the salt, baking powder, cinnamon, nutmeg, and almonds to the oats; mix well.

3. In a medium bowl, whisk together the milk, egg, vanilla, and maple syrup. Pour the custard mixture over the oats.

4. Melt the butter in the skillet, and swirl to coat the surface and sides. Add the fresh berries, and sprinkle with the brown sugar. Cook, stirring, just until the sugar dissolves.

5. Pour the oat mixture into the skillet, and transfer to the oven. Bake until set and golden, about 45 minutes.

6. Serve the oatmeal topped with warm milk and additional maple syrup and berries, if desired.

# COCONUT MILK FRENCH TOAST WITH CARAMELIZED PINEAPPLE

**2 (12") SKILLETS** / Vegetarian / Weekday

**Serves 4 / Prep time: 10 minutes / Cook time: 25 minutes**

This recipe was born in a rental condo during a Maui vacation. There wasn't much in the kitchen to work with, but there were eggs, sugar, cinnamon, and a can of coconut milk. I picked up some locally baked challah bread and the most perfect pineapple, and this French toast came to life.

### FOR THE FRENCH TOAST

4 large eggs

½ cup full-fat coconut milk

2 teaspoons sugar

1 teaspoon vanilla extract

½ teaspoon ground cinnamon

Pinch salt

Unsalted butter, for frying

8 challah bread slices

½ cup toasted shredded coconut (optional)

½ cup chopped toasted macadamia nuts (optional)

### FOR THE CARAMELIZED PINEAPPLE

⅓ cup sugar

2 tablespoons unsalted butter, plus more as needed

Half a large pineapple (about 2 cups), peeled, cored, and sliced

### TO MAKE THE FRENCH TOAST

1. Preheat a skillet over medium heat.

2. In a large bowl, whisk together the eggs, coconut milk, sugar, vanilla, cinnamon, and salt to make the custard.

3. Melt the butter (at least 2 tablespoons to start, adding more as needed) in the skillet. Dip the bread into the custard, giving each side a few seconds in the mixture and coating evenly. Immediately place the soaked bread in the skillet and cook, 2 slices at a time, until golden brown, 2 to 3 minutes per side. Melt more butter in the skillet and repeat with the remaining bread.

### TO MAKE THE CARAMELIZED PINEAPPLE AND SERVE

1. While the toast is cooking, preheat the other skillet over medium heat. Melt the butter in the skillet, and place the sugar in a shallow dish or plate.

2. Coat both sides of each pineapple slice in the sugar, then place the coated slices in the skillet in a single layer. (You might have to work in batches, adding more butter as needed.)

3. Cook until the pineapple begins to caramelize on one side, about 5 minutes. Carefully flip the pineapple slices over and continue cooking until softened and caramelized, 4 to 5 minutes.

4. Juice will release from the pineapple and form a lovely, golden caramel sauce. Top the French toast with the pineapple and sauce, and serve with the macadamia nuts and toasted coconut (if using).

**SUBSTITUTION TIP:** Make this recipe dairy-free by using coconut oil in place of butter.

# BANANA AND CHOCOLATE-HAZELNUT DUTCH BABY PANCAKE

**10" SKILLET** / One Pan / Vegetarian / Weekday

**Serves 4 / Prep time: 10 minutes / Cook time: 25 minutes**

A cast iron skillet is the perfect vessel for the classic Dutch baby. It gets the perimeter of the pancake perfectly golden and crispy while keeping the inside light and custardy. I especially enjoy this decadent version, with caramelized bananas and crunchy hazelnuts.

2 large eggs

½ cup buttermilk

½ cup all-purpose flour

2 tablespoons white sugar

½ teaspoon salt

¼ teaspoon ground cinnamon

½ teaspoon vanilla extract

2 tablespoons unsalted butter

1 large banana, thinly sliced, divided

1 tablespoon brown sugar

¼ cup chocolate-hazelnut spread

1 tablespoon whole milk, plus more if needed

¼ cup chopped hazelnuts

1. Preheat the oven to 425°F, and preheat the skillet over medium heat.

2. In a blender, combine the eggs, buttermilk, flour, white sugar, salt, cinnamon, and vanilla. Blend for 30 seconds, until smooth. Let the mixture stand for 10 minutes.

3. Meanwhile, melt the butter in the hot skillet, and swirl to coat the pan. Add half of the sliced banana and the brown sugar. Cook until lightly caramelized, about 3 minutes.

4. Pour the batter into the hot skillet and immediately transfer to the oven. Bake until puffed and golden, about 20 minutes. Do not open the oven while baking to prevent the pancake from collapsing.

5. In a small bowl in the microwave or a small pan over medium heat, melt the chocolate-hazelnut spread with the milk. Whisk until the mixture looks like a thick sauce, thinning it with more milk, if needed.

6. Drizzle the sauce on top of the Dutch baby, and sprinkle with hazelnuts and the remaining sliced banana. Cut into wedges and serve.

# HAWAIIAN BREAKFAST FRIED RICE

**12" SKILLET** / Weekday

**Serves 6 / Prep time: 10 minutes / Cook time: 30 minutes**

I've been lucky to spend quite a bit of time in Hawaii because my dad was stationed there. A typical Hawaiian breakfast is pretty simple, but there are a few things you'll always find on the menu, whether you're dining at a trendy tourist spot or a hole-in-the-wall. These include SPAM and eggs, macadamia nut pancakes, and acai bowls. But my favorite Hawaiian breakfast staple will always be fried rice. It typically has SPAM, ham, Portuguese sausage (linguica), and bacon. This version is simple to make, with easy-to-find ingredients.

5 thick-cut bacon slices, diced

1 sweet onion, diced

1 red bell pepper, diced

Salt

Freshly ground black pepper

1 (7-ounce) ham steak, cubed

2 garlic cloves, minced

1 cup chopped fresh pineapple

3 tablespoons soy sauce

1 tablespoon toasted sesame oil

1 tablespoon oyster sauce

1 tablespoon honey

2 teaspoons minced fresh ginger

4 cups cooked, day-old rice (brown or white)

3 tablespoons chopped scallions, green parts only

6 over-easy large fried eggs

1. Preheat the skillet over medium heat. Cook the bacon until crisp, about 8 minutes. Transfer to a paper towel–lined plate, reserving 2 tablespoons of bacon fat in the pan.

2. Add the onion to the hot pan and cook until translucent, 5 to 7 minutes. Add the bell pepper and cook until just tender, about 5 minutes. Season with salt and pepper.

3. Add the cubed ham to the pan and cook, in one even layer, until slightly browned and caramelized, about 5 minutes. Stir in the garlic and pineapple and cook for another 2 minutes.

4. In a small bowl, whisk together the soy sauce, sesame oil, oyster sauce, honey, and ginger. Add the rice to the pan and stir until everything is combined and heated through, about 3 minutes. Pour the sauce over the rice, and return the bacon to the pan.

5. Cook the fried rice until golden and slightly crispy in parts, another 2 to 3 minutes. Top each serving with scallions and an over-easy fried egg.

**COOKING TIP:** Substitute canned pineapple when fresh pineapple is out of season. You can also make a well in the skillet and scramble some whisked eggs right into the rice to make this a one-pan dish. However, in my opinion, the best part is when those runny yolks from an over-easy fried egg mix into the fried rice.

# SAVORY BREAKFAST BREAD PUDDING

**12" SKILLET** / One Pan

**Serves 6 to 8 / Prep time: 15 minutes / Cook time: 1 hour 10 minutes**

Bread pudding is a classic dessert. Here, it gets a savory twist for a hearty breakfast that can feed a crowd. Bread pudding is basically bread, milk, and eggs—three common morning staples. Adding bacon, breakfast sausage, and cheese makes for a rich and flavorful casserole that's perfect for weekend brunch.

5 thick-cut bacon slices, diced

½ yellow onion, diced

6 ounces turkey breakfast sausage, casings removed

2 garlic cloves, minced

2 cups baby spinach

Salt

Freshly ground black pepper

4 large eggs

2 cups whole milk

2 cups shredded Cheddar cheese

6 cups cubed (1-inch) sourdough bread

2 tablespoons unsalted butter

Chopped fresh parsley, for serving

1.  Preheat the oven to 350°F, and preheat the skillet over medium heat. Cook the diced bacon until crisp, about 6 minutes. Transfer the bacon to a paper towel-lined plate, reserving 1 tablespoon of bacon fat in the skillet. Add the onion and cook until translucent, 5 to 7 minutes.

2.  Add the turkey sausage to the skillet, using a wooden spoon to break it up. Cook the sausage until it is browned and cooked through, about 10 minutes. Stir in the garlic and spinach; cook until the spinach is just wilted. Season with salt and pepper. Transfer the mixture to a small bowl to cool.

3.  In a large bowl, whisk the eggs, milk, and Cheddar cheese. Put the cubed sourdough bread in a large bowl, and pour the egg mixture over top. Let sit for 10 minutes.

4.  Melt the butter in the still-hot skillet, and swirl to coat. Fold the sausage mixture and the cooked bacon into the bread pudding. Pour everything into the hot skillet, and transfer to the oven.

5.  Bake until the bread pudding is set and golden brown, 35 to 45 minutes. Serve topped with parsley.

# SPRING GREEN SHAKSHUKA

**12″ SKILLET** / Gluten-Free / Grain-Free / One Pan / Quick & Easy / Vegetarian

**Serves 6 / Prep time: 10 minutes / Cook time: 20 minutes**

Shakshuka is not only fun to say; it's delicious to eat. This green version utilizes all the beauty of fresh, seasonal spring produce. Part salad, part savory egg dish, this shakshuka is full of bright flavors, fresh herbs, and a little bit of heat.

2 tablespoons extra-virgin olive oil

1 leek, white and light green part only, halved lengthwise and thinly sliced

2 garlic cloves, minced

1 cup chopped asparagus

1 jalapeño pepper, thinly sliced

1 zucchini, sliced

2 cups chopped kale

Salt

Freshly ground black pepper

½ teaspoon ground coriander

½ teaspoon ground cumin

¼ teaspoon crushed Aleppo pepper

¼ cup vegetable stock

1 cup peas

2 cups baby spinach

6 large eggs

¼ cup chopped fresh mint

¼ cup chopped fresh parsley

¼ cup chopped fresh dill

4 radishes, thinly sliced

½ cup arugula

1.  Preheat the skillet over medium heat. Heat the olive oil, and add the leek. Cook until translucent, about 3 minutes, and stir in the garlic.

2.  Add the asparagus, jalapeño pepper, zucchini, and kale. Cook the vegetables until crisp-tender, about 5 minutes. Season with salt and pepper.

3.  Stir in the coriander, cumin, and Aleppo pepper. Add the vegetable stock, peas, and baby spinach. Cook until the vegetables are tender but still very green, about 3 minutes.

4.  Make 6 indentations in the vegetable mixture. Crack an egg into each indentation, and season with salt and pepper. Cover the skillet and cook until the egg whites are set but the yolks are soft, about 6 minutes.

5.  Turn off the heat and carefully stir in the fresh herbs. Top with the radish and arugula before serving.

**INGREDIENT TIP:** Aleppo pepper is a fruity, flavorful spice with a medium heat that is popular in Middle Eastern cuisine. Substitute hot paprika if you can't find it.

# SMOKED SALMON POTATO LATKES

**12″ SKILLET** / One Pan / Quick & Easy

**Serves 6 / Prep time: 10 minutes / Cook time: 20 minutes**

When I worked in Manhattan, I always looked forward to my Sunday morning lox bagel from the Jewish deli around the corner. I worked weekends (that's standard in the culinary world), but I actually loved working on Sundays. The bustling city always seemed quieter on Sundays, and during the early morning hours it sometimes felt like I had Chambers Street all to myself. I don't live on the East Coast anymore, so I make these smoked salmon–topped potato latkes whenever I feel homesick.

**FOR THE LATKES**

1 large russet potato, peeled and
   shredded (about 2 cups)

½ yellow onion, grated

1 large egg, beaten

2 tablespoons all-purpose flour

1 teaspoon salt

½ teaspoon freshly ground black pepper

¼ cup vegetable oil

**FOR SERVING**

½ cup whole-fat sour cream

1 tablespoon chopped fresh dill, plus
   more for serving

¼ teaspoon lemon zest

6 ounces smoked salmon

Scallions, green parts only, chopped

Capers

Lemon wedges

1.  Preheat the skillet over medium heat.

2.  Wring the shredded potato in cheesecloth to remove the water. In a medium bowl, mix the potato with the onion, egg, flour, salt, and pepper. Stir until the flour is absorbed.

3.  Heat the vegetable oil, and when it is hot, drop 4 scoops of the potato mixture into the pan, spacing them a few inches apart; use a spatula to lightly flatten each mound.

4.  Fry the latkes in batches of 4 until golden brown, 2 to 3 minutes per side. You should end up with 12 latkes total. Transfer them to a paper towel–lined plate to drain.

5.  In a small bowl, mix the sour cream with the chopped dill and lemon zest.

6.  To serve, spoon some sour cream on top of the latkes. Top with the smoked salmon, scallions, additional fresh dill, and some capers. Serve with lemon wedges.

**VARIATION TIP:** To make these latkes gluten-free, substitute rice flour for the flour.

# AVOCADO TOAST EGG IN A HOLE

**10″ SKILLET** / 5-Ingredient / One Pan / Quick & Easy / Vegetarian

**Serves 2 / Prep time: 5 minutes / Cook time: 5 minutes**

Whether you call it Egg in a Hole, Toad in a Hole, Egg in a Nest, or Bullseye Eggs—you know what it is, and that it's delicious. This is the first breakfast I ever made for my husband (who had never even heard of it before, which shocked me). Egg in a Hole is probably my favorite quick breakfast, with the close runner-up being avocado toast. So why not combine them?

2 thick sourdough bread slices

2 tablespoons unsalted butter

2 large eggs

Salt

Freshly ground black pepper

¼ cup grated smoked Gruyère cheese

1 avocado, thinly sliced or
   lightly mashed

Crushed red pepper flakes, for serving

1.  Preheat the skillet over medium heat. Using a biscuit cutter or the rim of a small glass, cut a hole in the center of each slice of bread. (Toast the round cutouts as well, or reserve them for bread crumbs.)

2.  Melt the butter in the skillet, and add the bread. Toast until the bottoms are golden, about 3 minutes.

3.  Flip the bread slices over, and crack the eggs into the center holes. Season with salt and pepper and let sizzle until the whites are set, the yolk is soft, and the other side of the bread is toasted, about 3 minutes more.

4.  Sprinkle with the Gruyère cheese and cover with a lid. Cook for another minute or so, until the egg whites are completely set and the cheese is melted.

5.  Serve each slice topped with half of the avocado and a pinch crushed red pepper flakes.

**VARIATION TIP:** You can get really creative with this recipe. Garnish it with fresh herbs like parsley, basil, or cilantro, or top with halved cherry tomatoes and a drizzle of balsamic. For a meatier breakfast, layer 2 slices of cooked bacon or turkey bacon on each egg toast before adding the avocado.

# EGGS IN PURGATORY WITH HARISSA, CHICKPEAS, AND FETA

**12" SKILLET** / Gluten-Free / Grain-Free / One Pan / Vegetarian

**Serves 6 / Prep time: 5 minutes / Cook time: 30 minutes**

This dish is fiery red, in both color and heat. It gets its spiciness from North African harissa paste and a Mediterranean spin from feta and cumin. Chickpeas add heartiness, and the tangy feta and bright cilantro help balance the spices. Adjust this dish to your preferred spice level by adding the harissa paste a teaspoon at a time.

2 tablespoons extra-virgin olive oil

1 yellow onion, diced

1 (15-ounce) can chickpeas, drained and rinsed

2 garlic cloves, minced

1 tablespoon tomato paste

2 tablespoons harissa paste

1 (28-ounce) can crushed or diced tomatoes, undrained

¾ cup sliced jarred roasted red peppers

Salt

Freshly ground black pepper

1 teaspoon smoked paprika

1 teaspoon ground cumin

6 large eggs

¼ cup chopped fresh cilantro

¾ cup crumbled feta cheese

1.  Preheat the skillet over medium heat. Heat the olive oil. Add the onion and cook until softened, about 5 minutes. Add the chickpeas and cook until they start to lightly brown in the oil, about 5 minutes. Stir in the garlic, tomato paste, and harissa paste. Cook for 2 minutes, until fragrant.

2.  Add the tomatoes with their juices and the roasted red peppers. Season with salt and pepper, and add the paprika and cumin.

3.  Let the tomato mixture simmer until thick and flavorful, about 10 minutes.

4.  Make 6 indentations in the sauce, and crack an egg into each. Top each egg with a pinch of salt and pepper. Cover the skillet and cook until the egg whites are set but the yolks are still soft, about 6 minutes. (Alternatively, you can pop the skillet in a 375°F oven for 8 minutes or so.)

5.  When the eggs are done, top with the cilantro and feta and serve.

**INGREDIENT TIP:** Harissa paste is made from hot peppers, herbs, and spices. If you don't have any, you can substitute with Sriracha or red pepper flakes.

# ORANGE-RICOTTA PANCAKES WITH AMARETTO CHERRY COMPOTE

**12″ SKILLET OR GRIDDLE** / One Pan / Vegetarian / Weekday

**Serves 2-4 / Prep time: 15 minutes / Cook time: 40 minutes**

I first ate lemon ricotta pancakes at Sarabeth's in New York City nearly a decade ago. A plate of those berry-topped pancakes paired with a St. Germain mimosa was my idea of heaven. I like using orange and cherries here instead of the popular lemon pairing.

## FOR THE COMPOTE

¼ cup freshly squeezed orange juice

¼ cup Amaretto

⅓ cup sugar

2 strips orange zest

1 cinnamon stick

2 cups pitted fresh or frozen (thawed) cherries, halved

## FOR THE PANCAKES

1 cup whole-milk ricotta

¾ cup buttermilk

1 teaspoon vanilla extract

2 tablespoons freshly squeezed orange juice

1 tablespoon freshly grated orange zest

2 large eggs, separated

1 cup all-purpose flour

¼ cup sugar

1 teaspoon baking powder

½ teaspoon salt

Unsalted butter, for cooking

Toasted almonds, chopped, for serving (optional)

### TO MAKE THE COMPOTE

In a small saucepan, combine the orange juice, Amaretto, sugar, orange zest, and cinnamon stick. Bring to a simmer over medium heat. Add the cherries and continue to simmer until the cherries are very soft and the liquid is syrupy, about 10 minutes. Remove from the heat and let cool slightly.

### TO MAKE THE PANCAKES

1. Preheat the skillet or griddle over medium heat. In a medium bowl, whisk together the ricotta, buttermilk, vanilla, orange juice, orange zest, and egg yolks.

2. In another medium bowl, whisk the flour, sugar, baking powder, and salt.

3. In a small bowl, beat the egg whites with a handheld electric mixer until soft peaks form, about 3 minutes.

4. Stir the flour mixture into the ricotta mixture in two additions, being careful not to overmix. Gently fold in the egg whites.

5. Butter the hot pan, and ladle in about one-eighth of the pancake batter for each pancake. The pan should accommodate 3 pancakes at a time.

6. Cook the first side until bubbles form on top and the bottom is golden, about 3 minutes. Flip and cook the second side until golden, about 2 minutes more. Transfer to a serving platter and tent with aluminum foil to keep warm. Repeat with the remaining batter.

7. Serve immediately, topped with the warm compote and toasted almonds.

**VARIATION TIP:** These pancakes are just as good topped with maple syrup and powdered sugar. Skip making the compote, if you like, and top with seasonal fruit instead.

# BACON-JAM BREAKFAST BLTS

**10″ SKILLET** / One Pan / Weekday

Serves 4 / Prep time: 10 minutes / Cook time: 25 minutes

Bacon jam may sound fancy, but it takes very little effort. Bacon combines with onion, garlic, bourbon, and maple syrup to create a sweet-and-salty, sticky jam that takes your everyday BLT to the next level. Adding a perfectly fried egg makes for a very satisfying breakfast.

**FOR THE BACON JAM**

8 ounces bacon, diced

1 medium shallot, finely diced

1 small yellow onion, finely diced

Salt

Freshly ground black pepper

1 garlic clove, minced

3 tablespoons apple cider vinegar

2 tablespoons maple syrup

2 tablespoons bourbon

3 tablespoons brown sugar

½ teaspoon paprika

½ teaspoon chili powder

**FOR THE SANDWICHES**

Mayonnaise, for spreading

8 bread slices or 4 English muffins, toasted

4 large fried eggs

Tomato, sliced

Romaine or butter lettuce, torn

Avocado, thinly sliced

Salt

Freshly ground black pepper

### TO MAKE THE BACON JAM

1. Preheat the skillet over medium heat. Sauté the bacon until crisp, 6 to 8 minutes. Transfer the bacon to a paper towel–lined plate to drain, leaving 2 tablespoons of bacon fat in the pan.

2. Add the shallot and onion and cook over medium-low heat until they start to caramelize, 5 to 7 minutes. Season with salt and pepper, and add the garlic.

3. Return the bacon to the pan and add the vinegar, maple syrup, bourbon, brown sugar, paprika, and chili powder. Stir until combined. Allow the mixture to come to a simmer, then turn the heat to low. Cook the bacon jam, stirring often, until all the liquid is evaporated, about 10 minutes.

### TO ASSEMBLE THE SANDWICHES

Spread a thin layer of mayonnaise on toasted bread or English muffins. Spoon some of the bacon jam onto each piece of bread; spread evenly. On each of 4 bread slices, layer a fried egg, several tomato slices, some lettuce, and a few avocado slices. Season with salt and pepper, top with another bread slice, and serve.

**VARIATION TIP:** Instead of spreading the classic mayo on these sandwiches, try adding a thin layer of savory cream cheese.

*Pumpkin Cinnamon Rolls
with Spiced Cream Cheese
page 48*

# chapter three

# BISCUITS & BREAD

# HONEY-BACON CORNBREAD

**10" SKILLET** / One Pan / Weeknight

**Serves 8 / Prep time: 10 minutes / Cook time: 35 minutes**

I was tasked with making cornbread at one of my first professional pastry jobs. One morning, I forgot the leavening ingredients, resulting in thin, sad-looking cornbread. I quickly made a new batch and set the first batch aside. Later that day, I sandwiched crispy bacon and a Cheddar-topped fried egg in the flat cornbread, and, drizzled the tops with warm honey, and served the treat to the staff. All was forgiven. This sweet-and-savory cornbread is inspired by that happy accident.

6 applewood-smoked bacon slices, finely chopped

1 cup medium-ground yellow cornmeal

1 cup all-purpose flour

2 tablespoons sugar

½ teaspoon salt

3 teaspoons baking powder

¼ teaspoon baking soda

2 large eggs

1 cup buttermilk

8 tablespoons (1 stick) unsalted butter, melted

⅓ cup honey, plus more for serving

1. Preheat the oven to 400°F.

2. Preheat the skillet over medium heat. Cook the bacon until crispy, about 6 minutes. Transfer the bacon to a paper towel–lined plate, reserving 1 tablespoon of bacon fat in the pan.

3. While the bacon cooks, in a large bowl, whisk together the cornmeal, flour, sugar, salt, baking powder, and baking soda. In a medium bowl, whisk together the eggs, buttermilk, melted butter, and honey.

4. Pour the wet mixture into the dry, and stir until just combined. Fold in the bacon.

5. Swirl the tablespoon of bacon fat around to coat the pan, and pour the batter into the warm skillet.

6. Bake until the cornbread is golden and a tester inserted into the center comes out clean, 22 to 25 minutes. Serve warm with a drizzle of honey.

**SUBSTITUTION TIP:** Don't have buttermilk? Stir 1 tablespoon of lemon juice into 1 cup of whole milk, and let it stand for 10 minutes before using.

# OLIVE-ROSEMARY FOCACCIA

**10″ SKILLET** / 5-Ingredient / One Pan / Vegan

**Serves 8 / Prep time: 30 minutes, plus 2 to 3 hours to rise / Cook time: 15 minutes**

If you've never dealt with yeast before, focaccia is a great place to start. Making it in cast iron ensures it produces a crisp, golden crust with the most tender interior.

1 cup warm (105 to 115°F) water

1 teaspoon sugar

1½ teaspoons active dry yeast

2 cups all-purpose flour, plus more
  for dusting

1 teaspoon salt

½ cup extra-virgin olive oil, divided

1 tablespoon chopped fresh rosemary

18 pitted kalamata olives, halved

1. In a small bowl, combine the warm water, sugar, and yeast. Let the mixture sit until foamy, 10 to 15 minutes.

2. In the bowl of a standing electric mixer fitted with the bread hook, combine the flour and salt. Add ¼ cup of olive oil and the yeast mixture. Mix for about 6 minutes, until the dough is smooth and elastic.

3. Place the dough on a floured surface and knead it a few times. Put the dough in a lightly greased bowl, cover with a damp cloth, and place in a warm spot. Let the dough rise for 1 to 2 hours, until doubled in size.

4. Place 2 tablespoons of olive oil in the bottom of the skillet. Place the focaccia dough on top of that, and, using your fingers, flatten, stretch, and spread the dough out to the edges. Cover the dough again and place it in a warm spot for 1 hour, until doubled.

5. Preheat the oven to 450°F.

6. Create small "dimples" in the focaccia bread with your fingertips. Drizzle the remaining 2 tablespoons of olive oil on top, along with the chopped rosemary. Season with salt, and lay the olive halves on top.

7. Bake until golden, about 15 minutes. Serve warm or at room temperature.

**COOKING TIP:** When proofing yeast, make sure the water is between 105 and 115°F, around the temperature of a hot bath. If the water is too hot, the yeast will die; if it's too cold, the yeast will not grow.

# ROASTED GARLIC OIL NAAN

**12" SKILLET, MINI COCOTTE** / Vegetarian

**Serves 8 / Prep time: 30 minutes, plus 1 hour to rise / Cook time: 25 minutes**

Indian food is a takeout staple in our home. I always change up my order, but one thing is a must: naan. The naan from our favorite Indian restaurant is larger than our dog and arrives folded over itself four times in a giant paper shopping bag. This delicious naan features an incredibly easy-to-make garlic-infused oil.

**FOR THE GARLIC OIL**

¼ cup extra-virgin olive oil

8 garlic cloves, peeled and smashed

**FOR THE NAAN**

1 (0.25-ounce) packet active dry yeast

½ cup warm (105 to 115°F) water

2 teaspoons honey

½ cup warm whole milk

⅓ cup plain, whole-fat yogurt

3¼ cups all-purpose flour, plus more for dusting

½ teaspoon salt

Extra-virgin olive oil, for greasing

### TO MAKE THE GARLIC OIL

Preheat the oven to 350°F. In a mini cocotte or small, oven-safe dish, combine the olive oil with the garlic cloves. Bake for 12 to 15 minutes, until the garlic is golden and fragrant. Let cool.

### TO MAKE THE NAAN

1. In a small bowl, combine the yeast, warm water, and honey. Let the mixture sit until foamy, 10 to 15 minutes.

2. In a medium bowl, whisk the milk with the yogurt. In a large bowl, whisk together the flour and salt.

3.  When the yeast mixture is ready, whisk it into the milk and yogurt mixture. Make a well in the center of the flour, and pour the wet ingredients in. Stir until the mixture comes together.

4.  Turn the dough out onto a lightly floured surface; knead with floured hands until smooth and elastic. If the dough is too sticky, add a bit more flour.

5.  When the dough comes together, form it into a ball and place in a lightly oiled bowl. Cover with a damp towel or plastic wrap, and let sit in a warm place until roughly doubled in size, about 1 hour.

6.  Preheat the skillet over medium-high heat. Transfer your dough onto a floured surface and roll it into a rough log. Cut the log into 8 equal pieces.

7.  Roll out each piece into a flat oval or round measuring about 1/4 inch thick.

8.  Cook one naan in the hot skillet until bubbles form on one side, about 2 minutes. Flip and cook for another minute or so, until browned and golden in spots.

9.  Brush with the garlic oil and sprinkle with sea salt while the naan is still warm, and repeat with the remaining dough pieces.

**SERVING TIP:** Serve this naan with Cauliflower and Potato Curry (Aloo Gobi) (page 86) or use it to make quick individual pizzas. This naan is also delicious grilled.

# SKILLET WHISKEY IRISH SODA BREAD

**8″ SKILLET** / **One Pan** / **Vegetarian**

**Serves 8 / Prep time: 25 minutes / Cook time: 45 minutes**

Each year on St. Patrick's Day, my mom and I go on a mission to find the best Irish soda bread. Growing up in New Jersey, I could always find freshly baked soda bread easily. It became harder when we moved to the West Coast, so I started making my own. The cast iron skillet helps it develop a beautifully golden, rustic crust.

**FOR THE BREAD**

½ cup raisins

2 tablespoons whiskey

2 tablespoons honey

1 cup buttermilk

2 cups all-purpose flour, plus more
   for dusting

1 teaspoon baking powder

½ teaspoon baking soda

1 teaspoon salt

2 tablespoons cold unsalted butter

1 tablespoon melted unsalted butter

1 tablespoon sugar

**FOR THE WHISKEY-HONEY BUTTER
   (OPTIONAL)**

8 tablespoons (1 stick) unsalted butter,
   at room temperature

1 tablespoon whiskey (reserved from
   the raisins)

2 tablespoons honey

Pinch salt

## TO MAKE THE BREAD

1. Preheat the oven to 400°F.

2. Place the raisins in a small heat-proof bowl. In a microwave-safe mug in the microwave or in a small saucepan over medium-high heat, heat the whiskey until very hot but not boiling. Pour it over the raisins. Let sit for 20 minutes, until the raisins soak up half of the whiskey. Use a fork or slotted spoon to remove the raisins from the bowl, reserving the leftover whiskey for the butter, if using.

3. Meanwhile, in a small bowl, whisk together the honey and buttermilk. In a large bowl, whisk together the flour, baking powder, baking soda, and salt.

4. Using a pastry cutter or fork, cut the cold butter into the flour mixture until the butter is broken into small, pea-size pieces. Stir in the raisins. Make a well in the center of the flour. Pour the honey and buttermilk mixture into the well; stir it into the flour until just combined.

5. Transfer the dough to a floured surface. Gently knead and shape it into a round ball.

6. Grease the skillet with butter and place the soda bread in it. Using a sharp knife, cut an "X" on the top of the bread. Brush the melted butter over the surface, and sprinkle with the sugar.

7. Transfer to the oven and bake until golden brown and cooked through, 40 to 45 minutes. Serve warm with a generous amount of butter or whiskey-honey butter.

### TO MAKE THE WHISKEY-HONEY BUTTER (IF USING)

Beat the softened butter with the whiskey and honey until combined and lightly whipped. Season with salt.

**INGREDIENT TIP:** If you prefer not to make this bread with whiskey, plump the raisins with warmed apple juice instead.

# PUMPKIN CINNAMON ROLLS WITH SPICED CREAM CHEESE

**12" SKILLET, SMALL POT** / Vegetarian

Serves 8 / Prep time: 45 minutes, plus 2 hours 30 minutes to rise / Cook time: 20 minutes

My husband, Ryan, is a cinnamon roll fiend. There aren't many gas stations he'll come out of without a wrapped cinnamon roll in hand. When I first made these pumpkin rolls, he took a bite and his eyes lit up like a Christmas tree. These rolls are perfect to make during the fall and winter and are laced with plenty of warm, fragrant spices.

**FOR THE ROLLS**

1 tablespoon honey

¼ cup warm (105 to 115°F) water

1 (.25-ounce) packet active dry yeast

½ cup buttermilk

8 tablespoons (1 stick) unsalted butter

¾ cup pumpkin purée

3½ cups all-purpose flour, plus more for dusting

1 tablespoon pumpkin pie spice

¼ cup sugar

1 teaspoon salt

1 large egg, beaten

**FOR THE FILLING**

6 tablespoons (¾ stick) unsalted butter, at room temperature

1 cup brown sugar

1 teaspoon ground cinnamon

½ teaspoon ground ginger

¼ teaspoon ground nutmeg

Baking spray or more unsalted butter, for greasing

**FOR THE ICING**

4 ounces whole-fat cream cheese, at room temperature

2 tablespoons unsalted butter, at room temperature

1½ cups confectioners' sugar

½ teaspoon vanilla extract

½ teaspoon ground cinnamon

⅛ teaspoon ground nutmeg

2 to 3 tablespoons whole milk

*TO MAKE THE ROLLS*

1. In a small bowl, dissolve the honey in the warm water, then sprinkle in the yeast. Let sit until the yeast is foamy, 10 to 15 minutes.

2. Meanwhile, in a small pot, heat the buttermilk and butter until the butter is melted. Remove from the heat and stir in the pumpkin purée.

3. In the bowl of a standing mixer fitted with the bread hook, whisk together the flour, pumpkin pie spice, sugar, and salt.

4. Add the yeast mixture, buttermilk mixture, and beaten egg to the flour. Mix for 7 minutes, until a smooth dough ball forms. Transfer the dough to an oiled bowl, cover with a damp towel, and place in a warm spot. Let the dough rise for 1 to 1½ hours.

5. When the dough has risen, punch it down and flip it onto a well-floured counter-top. Sprinkle flour over the top, and roll the dough into a large rectangle, roughly 15 by 12 inches.

6. Spread the softened butter evenly over the entire rectangle. In a small bowl, mix together the brown sugar, cinnamon, ginger, and nutmeg, and sprinkle evenly over the butter.

7. Roll the dough tightly, starting from the longest side of the rectangle. Using a sharp knife, trim each end of your log. Cut the dough log in half, and cut each half into 4 even slices to make 8 rolls.

8. Grease your cast iron pan very well with baking spray or butter. Arrange the sliced rolls in the skillet with 7 around the edges and 1 in the center. Cover with the damp towel, and let rise in a warm place for another hour, until doubled in size.

9. Preheat the oven to 375°F.

10. Once the rolls have risen, bake them in the oven until golden, puffed, and cooked through, 22 to 25 minutes. If the rolls are becoming too dark, cover them with foil for the last 5 minutes.

### TO MAKE THE ICING AND SERVE

1. In a medium bowl, beat together the cream cheese and butter with a handhand mixer. Beat in the sugar, little by little, until combined. Add the vanilla, cinnamon, and nutmeg. Beat in the milk to your desired consistency.

2. Spread the cinnamon rolls with the icing and serve warm.

**COOKING TIP:** You can prepare these cinnamon rolls the night before and bake them fresh the next morning. Follow the recipe through step 7, then chill the sliced rolls in the refrigerator overnight. The next day, let the rolls come to room tempera-ture and rise in a warm place for at least an hour, until doubled in size, before baking.

# SKILLET SOUR CREAM COFFEE CAKE WITH WALNUT STREUSEL

**10″ SKILLET** / One Pan / Vegetarian / Weeknight

Serves 10 / Prep time: 15 minutes / Cook time: 45 minutes

There's nothing quite like a warm slice of coffee cake with your morning cup of coffee. This skillet coffee cake is moist and tender, and studded inside and out with a nutty streusel. It's perfect for a weekend brunch, and serving it in the cast iron skillet keeps it warm for longer.

**FOR THE STREUSEL**

½ cup all-purpose flour

½ cup brown sugar

2 teaspoons ground cinnamon

4 tablespoons (½ stick) cold unsalted butter, cut into small pieces

1 cup finely chopped walnuts

Pinch salt

**FOR THE COFFEE CAKE**

¾ cup unsalted butter, at room temperature

1½ cups sugar

¾ cup whole-fat sour cream

2 large eggs

1 teaspoon vanilla extract

1¾ cups all-purpose flour

1 teaspoon baking powder

¼ teaspoon baking soda

½ teaspoon salt

Baking spray or more unsalted butter, for greasing

### TO MAKE THE STREUSEL

In a medium bowl, mix together the flour, brown sugar, and cinnamon. Using a pastry cutter or fork, cut in the cold butter until it is broken up into small, pea-size pieces. Stir in the walnuts and salt.

### TO MAKE THE COFFEE CAKE

1. Preheat the oven to 350°F.

2. In a medium bowl using a handheld mixer or in the bowl of a standing mixer, beat the butter with the sugar until light and fluffy. Beat in the sour cream, then the eggs, one at a time, and then the vanilla.

3. In a medium bowl, combine the flour, baking powder, baking soda, and salt. Add the flour mixture to the butter–sour cream mixture in two additions, and mix until just incorporated.

4. Grease the skillet very well with baking spray or butter. Spread half of the batter on the bottom of the pan. Sprinkle half of the streusel evenly on top. Spread the other half of the batter evenly on top of the streusel. Top with the remaining streusel.

5. Bake until a tester inserted into the center comes out clean and the streusel is golden brown, 40 to 45 minutes. Slice and serve.

**VARIATION TIP:** If you're not a fan of walnuts, you can try pecans and almonds. Both work well here.

# SWEET POTATO BISCUITS WITH MAPLE BUTTER

**12" SKILLET** / One Pan / Quick & Easy / Vegetarian

**Serves 8 / Prep time: 15 minutes / Cook time: 15 minutes**

These home-style biscuits get a golden, flaky crust while the addition of sweet potato keeps the inside tender with a pleasing peachy hue. These are delicious with maple butter, served at Thanksgiving dinner, or turned into ham or bacon and egg sandwiches.

## FOR THE BISCUITS

2 cups plus 2 tablespoons all-purpose
   flour, plus more for dusting

2 tablespoons brown sugar

1 teaspoon salt

1 tablespoon baking powder

½ teaspoon baking soda

8 tablespoons (1 stick) cold unsalted
   butter, cut into cubes

¾ cup puréed sweet potato

¾ cup buttermilk

Baking spray or more unsalted butter,
   for greasing

## FOR THE MAPLE BUTTER (OPTIONAL)

8 tablespoons (1 stick) unsalted butter,
   at room temperature

3 tablespoons maple syrup

¼ teaspoon ground cinnamon

Pinch salt

## TO MAKE THE BISCUITS

1. Preheat the oven to 425°F.

2. In a large bowl, combine the flour, brown sugar, salt, baking powder, and baking soda. Using a pastry cutter or fork, cut the butter into the flour until it is broken up into pea-size pieces.

3. In a medium bowl, whisk together the sweet potato purée and buttermilk. Make a well in the center of the flour and pour in the buttermilk mixture. Stir until just combined.

4. Turn the dough out onto a floured surface, and knead gently to just combine. Pat down or gently roll the dough into a 1-inch-thick disc.

5. Using a floured biscuit cutter, cut out 8 biscuits, re-rolling the first scraps only once.

6. Grease the skillet very well with baking spray or butter. Arrange the biscuits in the skillet and bake until golden, about 15 minutes.

**TO MAKE THE MAPLE BUTTER (IF USING) AND SERVE**

In a small bowl, combine the butter, maple syrup, cinnamon, and salt; beat, using a handheld or electric mixer, until the butter is light and fluffy. Serve the biscuits with the maple butter.

**COOKING TIP:** To make sweet potato purée, peel and dice a large sweet potato. Place the diced sweet potato in a pot and cover with water. Bring the water to a boil and cook until the potatoes are fork-tender, about 20 minutes. Drain the potatoes, then purée using a fork or potato masher until completely free of lumps.

# EVERYTHING BAGEL DINNER ROLLS

**12″ SKILLET** / One Pan / Vegetarian

Serves 12 / Prep time: 45 minutes, plus 2 hours 15 minutes to rise and sit / Cook time: 20 minutes

A dinner roll can be the ideal supper accessory—spread with butter, used for sopping up sauce, or split to sandwich small morsels of sweet ham or pot roast. I like to top these simple, minimal-ingredient dinner rolls with everything bagel seasoning, which can be found in stores or quickly made at home.

½ cup warm (105 to 115°F) water

2 tablespoons honey

1 (.25-ounce) packet active dry yeast

3½ cups all-purpose flour, plus more as needed

1 cup warm whole milk

4 tablespoons (½ stick) unsalted butter, at room temperature, plus more for brushing

1 large egg

1½ teaspoons salt

Vegetable oil, for greasing

¼ cup everything bagel seasoning (see tip)

1. In a small bowl, combine the warm water and honey. Sprinkle the yeast over top and let it sit until foamy, 10 to 15 minutes.

2. In the bowl of a standing mixer fitted with the bread hook, combine the flour, milk, butter, egg, salt, and yeast mixture.

3. Mix the dough until it comes together to form a smooth, elastic ball. It should be slightly sticky. If it is too wet, add more flour, tablespoon by tablespoon. Transfer to an oiled bowl, cover with a damp towel or plastic, and let rise in a warm place until doubled in size, about 1 hour.

4. Turn the dough out onto a floured surface and divide it into 12 equal pieces. Using floured hands, roll the pieces of dough in your hands to form balls. Arrange them in a greased skillet. Cover the skillet with a damp towel or plastic, and set it aside in a warm spot for 30 minutes to 1 hour, until the dough balls have doubled in size.

5. Preheat the oven to 375°F.

6. When the rolls are ready to be baked, brush them with butter and sprinkle each with some of the everything bagel seasoning.

7. Bake until golden brown, 18 to 20 minutes. Serve warm.

**INGREDIENT TIP:** You can buy everything bagel seasoning in the spice section at Trader Joe's. To make your own, combine 1 tablespoon poppy seeds, 1 tablespoon sesame seeds, 1 tablespoon dried garlic flakes, 1 tablespoon dried onion flakes, and 1½ teaspoons salt.

# SPICY JALAPEÑO-CHEDDAR BEER BREAD

**10" SKILLET, SMALL POT** / Vegetarian

Serves 10 / Prep time: 15 minutes / Cook time: 50 minutes

One of my favorite stands at the local farmers' market sells incredible pickled and candied peppers. I buy several jars of their sweet jalapeños each visit. One night I decided to add these peppers to beer bread, and the result was delicious. Cheesy, slightly spicy, and flavorful, beer bread baked in a cast iron skillet yields that crunchy, golden crust that we all know is the best part.

1 tablespoon extra-virgin olive oil

1 small shallot, minced

2 garlic cloves, minced

4 tablespoons (½ stick) unsalted butter, plus more for greasing

2 tablespoons honey

2½ cups all-purpose flour

1 teaspoon salt

2 teaspoons baking powder

1 cup shredded Cheddar cheese, divided

¾ cup chopped pickled jalapeño peppers, divided

12 ounces lager beer, at room temperature

1. Preheat the oven to 350°F.

2. Preheat the skillet over medium heat, and heat the olive oil. Add the shallot and cook until soft and golden, about 5 minutes. Stir in the garlic, and cook for another minute. Remove from the heat.

3. In a small pot over medium heat, melt the butter and honey.

4. In a large bowl, whisk together the flour, salt, and baking powder. Stir in ¾ cup of cheese and ½ cup of jalapeño peppers. Stir in the shallot and garlic.

5. Make a well in the center of the flour, and pour in the butter and room temperature beer. Stir until everything is just combined; do not overmix. The batter will be soft and sticky.

6. Grease the skillet with butter, and pour the batter into the pan. Spread evenly and top with the remaining ¼ cup of Cheddar and ¼ cup of chopped jalapeño peppers.

7. Bake until golden brown and cooked through, 35 to 45 minutes. Serve warm.

**INGREDIENT TIP:** To make this bread more mellow in heat, use only ⅓ cup of jalapeño peppers.

# SKILLET OLIVE OIL ZUCCHINI BREAD

**12" SKILLET** / One Pan / Vegetarian / Weeknight

Serves 12 / Prep time: 15 minutes / Cook time: 30 minutes

This is hands down the best zucchini bread I've ever had. The secret is the fruity olive oil and sour cream, which both help keep it moist. Or maybe it's the warm, fragrant spices or the toasted walnuts or floral honey. And then there's the cast iron skillet, which bakes this bread so evenly and yields a deeply golden crust.

Unsalted butter, for greasing

⅓ cup whole-fat sour cream

½ cup extra-virgin olive oil

½ cup packed brown sugar

¼ cup honey

2 large eggs

1½ cups all-purpose flour

½ teaspoon baking soda

½ teaspoon baking powder

1 teaspoon salt

½ teaspoon ground cinnamon

½ teaspoon ground ginger

¼ teaspoon ground nutmeg

½ cup chopped walnuts

1½ cups grated zucchini

1. Preheat the oven to 350°F, and butter the skillet.

2. In a large bowl, whisk together the sour cream, olive oil, brown sugar, and honey. Whisk in the eggs until everything is well incorporated.

3. In a medium bowl, whisk together the flour, baking soda, baking powder, salt, cinnamon, ginger, and nutmeg.

4. Stir the flour mixture into the wet mixture, and mix until just combined. Stir in the walnuts and zucchini.

5. Pour the mixture into the skillet and smooth the top. Bake until golden brown and a tester inserted into the center comes out clean, about 30 minutes. Serve warm or at room temperature.

**STORAGE TIP:** Wrap any leftover bread tightly in aluminum foil and store it at room temperature for 1 to 2 days or in the refrigerator for up to 4 days. If storing bread in the refrigerator, allow it to come to room temperature or gently toast or warm it before serving.

Moroccan Honey-Roasted
Carrots with Pistachios
page 64

# chapter four
## VEGETABLES & SIDES

# FENNEL-ARTICHOKE GRATIN

**10" SKILLET** / One Pan / Quick & Easy / Vegetarian

**Serves 4 / Prep time: 5 minutes / Cook time: 25 minutes**

Cast iron skillets are the perfect vessel for gratins. They allow for stove-top-to-oven cooking and great caramelization and browning. Sweet fennel and tender artichokes are the star of this show, with wine, garlic, cream, and Gruyère as the supporting acts. Crowned with a buttery, crisp crust, this elegant side dish is surprisingly simple to make when using frozen artichoke hearts.

1 tablespoon unsalted butter

1 tablespoon extra-virgin olive oil

1 fennel bulb, halved, cored, and sliced

1 pound frozen artichoke hearts, thawed
  and rinsed

2 garlic cloves, minced

¼ cup white wine

1 cup half-and-half

½ cup Gruyère cheese

Pinch ground nutmeg

Salt

Freshly ground black pepper

½ cup panko bread crumbs

½ cup Parmesan cheese

¼ teaspoon paprika

2 tablespoons unsalted butter, melted

3 tablespoons chopped fresh parsley

1.  Preheat the oven to 450°F, and preheat the skillet over medium heat.

2.  In the hot pan, melt the butter and heat the olive oil. Stir in the fennel. Cook until slightly caramelized and crisp-tender, about 3 minutes. Stir in the artichokes and garlic and cook for another 3 minutes, until the artichokes are just tender.

3.  Deglaze the pan with the white wine, using a wooden spoon to scrape up the browned bits from the bottom, and let it simmer for another minute. Stir in the half-and-half, Gruyère cheese, and nutmeg, and season with salt and pepper. Let the mixture just come to a simmer. Remove the pan from the heat.

4.  In a medium bowl, stir together the panko, Parmesan cheese, paprika, and melted butter. Top the artichokes with the bread crumbs, and transfer to the oven.

5.  Bake until golden, crisp, and bubbling, 10 to 12 minutes. Serve topped with the fresh parsley.

**INGREDIENT TIP:** When preparing fennel, keep the lacy fronds on the top stalks. Chop them and use them as a garnish.

# BRUSSELS SPROUTS WITH BACON AND HONEY-BALSAMIC GLAZE

**12" SKILLET** / 5-Ingredient / Gluten-Free / Grain-Free / One Pan / Weeknight

**Serves 4 / Prep time: 10 minutes / Cook time: 35 minutes**

I know my fair share of Brussels sprouts haters, but even those who hate them love this dish. It's likely because bacon is included, but I think the fruity honey and balsamic vinegar play big parts, too. This dish is especially superb when roasted in cast iron, which perfectly chars the sprouts and gives the leaves nice, crispy little edges.

4 bacon slices, diced

1 pound Brussels sprouts, trimmed
   and halved

1 tablespoon extra-virgin olive oil

Salt

Freshly ground black pepper

2 tablespoons balsamic vinegar

1 tablespoon honey

1.  Preheat the oven to 400°F, and preheat the skillet over medium heat.

2.  Cook the bacon until crispy, 6 to 8 minutes. Transfer the bacon to a paper towel–lined plate, leaving 1 tablespoon of bacon fat in the skillet.

3.  Add the Brussels sprouts to the hot skillet, and toss with the bacon fat and olive oil. Season with salt and pepper, and transfer to the oven. Roast the Brussels sprouts for 20 minutes, until tender and browned.

4.  Meanwhile, in a small bowl, whisk the balsamic vinegar and honey together.

5.  Remove the skillet from the oven and stir in the balsamic-honey mixture and the reserved bacon. Return the skillet to the oven to heat for 5 more minutes, then remove from the oven and serve.

**SUBSTITUTION TIP:** This dish is still delicious without the bacon, if you'd like to make it vegetarian. Just use 2 tablespoons of olive oil instead of 1, since you won't be using the bacon fat.

# ROSEMARY-PARSNIP POMMES ANNA WITH GOAT CHEESE

**12″ & 10″ SKILLET** / 5-Ingredient / Gluten-Free / Grain-Free / One Pan / Vegetarian

**Serves 8 / Prep time: 20 minutes / Cook time: 45 minutes**

Talk about a stunning dish. Pommes Anna is a classic French recipe dating back to the nineteenth century. Layers upon layers of thinly sliced potatoes are arranged in overlapping circles, with copious amounts of butter. This spin on the classic includes sliced parsnips, along with rosemary and goat cheese, which impart earthy, creamy, and slightly tangy notes. Yes, this recipe is a labor of love, but with a mandoline and a little time, it's a dish that impresses everyone.

Baking spray or unsalted butter, for greasing

3 russet potatoes (3 pounds), peeled

2 large parsnips (1½ pounds), peeled

Salt

Freshly ground black pepper

2 garlic cloves, minced, divided

1 tablespoon finely chopped fresh rosemary, divided, plus more for serving

4 ounces goat cheese, divided

8 tablespoons (1 stick) unsalted butter, melted

1. Preheat the oven to 425°F, and grease the skillet very well with baking spray or butter.

2. Using a mandoline slicer on the thinnest setting, slice the potatoes and transfer them to a large bowl of cold water. Slice the parsnips the same way and set aside.

3. Remove the potatoes from the water and drain them on layers of paper towels. Pat dry. On the bottom of the skillet, arrange one layer of potato slices in overlapping concentric circles. Brush evenly with some of the melted butter, and season with salt and pepper. Sprinkle evenly with about one-sixth of the garlic, rosemary, and goat cheese.

4. On top of the potatoes, arrange one layer of parsnips in overlapping concentric circles. Brush each layer with butter and season it with salt and pepper, along with one-sixth of the garlic, rosemary, and goat cheese.

5. Repeat this process for a total of 7 layers: 4 layers of potato and 3 layers of parsnips, with potato on the bottom and top.

6. Brush the remaining melted butter on the top layer, and season with salt and pepper.

7. Spray a large piece of aluminum foil liberally with baking spray, and place it on top of the potatoes, greased-side down. Place a 10-inch cast iron pan on top to weight down the Pommes Anna.

8. Bake, covered, for 20 minutes.

9. Remove the top pan and foil and continue to bake, uncovered, for 25 minutes more, until the top is golden and the potatoes are tender. A knife inserted into the center should go through easily.

10. Remove from the oven and let cool for several minutes. Slice and serve with additional fresh rosemary on top.

**SUBSTITUTION TIP:** Not a goat cheese fan? You can use freshly grated Parmesan or Gruyère cheeses instead.

# MOROCCAN HONEY-ROASTED CARROTS WITH PISTACHIOS

**12″ SKILLET** / Gluten-Free / Grain-Free / One Pan / Quick & Easy / Vegetarian

**Serves 4 / Prep time: 5 minutes / Cook time: 25 minutes**

Roasted rainbow carrots are gorgeous as is, especially when they're presented in cast iron. But these Moroccan jewel-tone carrots are even more lovely when topped with a lemon-yogurt drizzle and bright green pistachios. This is a side dish that looks as good as it tastes. Moroccan-inspired spices combine with floral honey and a touch of heat from Aleppo pepper to make these caramelized carrots sing.

1 pound small (3-inch) rainbow carrots, peeled and halved lengthwise

1½ tablespoons extra-virgin olive oil

1½ tablespoons honey

¾ teaspoon ground cumin

¼ teaspoon smoked paprika

¼ teaspoon crushed Aleppo pepper

Salt

Freshly ground black pepper

¼ cup plain, whole-fat yogurt

2 tablespoons freshly squeezed lemon juice

¼ cup chopped toasted pistachios

1. Preheat the oven to 425°F.

2. In the skillet, combine the carrots, olive oil, honey, cumin, paprika, and Aleppo pepper. Season with salt and pepper, and toss everything to coat evenly.

3. Transfer the skillet to the oven and roast until the carrots are caramelized, tender, and browned, 20 to 25 minutes. Stir the carrots halfway through.

4. In a small bowl, stir together the yogurt and lemon juice until combined. Season with salt and pepper. Drizzle the yogurt sauce over the roasted carrots, sprinkle with the chopped pistachios, and serve.

**INGREDIENT TIP:** You can substitute hot paprika and a pinch of crushed red pepper flakes for the Aleppo pepper.

# SESAME AND GARLIC ASPARAGUS WITH TAHINI SAUCE

**14" SKILLET** / Gluten-Free / Grain-Free / One Pan / Quick & Easy / Vegan

**Serves 4 / Prep time: 10 minutes / Cook time: 15 minutes**

Even though asparagus is one of my favorite vegetables, it can get quite boring after a while. We always make it the same way: roasted or grilled with lemon and olive oil. Delicious, but sometimes I want to change things up. After noticing how much I love asparagus in my stir-fries and how well it pairs with sesame, I created this tahini-topped side dish. It is definitely a great way to switch up your everyday asparagus routine.

| | |
|---|---|
| 1 pound asparagus, trimmed | 3 tablespoons tahini |
| 2 tablespoons extra-virgin olive oil | 2 tablespoons freshly squeezed |
| Salt | lemon juice |
| Freshly ground black pepper | 2 tablespoons warm water |
| 3 garlic cloves, minced | ¼ teaspoon garlic powder |
| 2 teaspoons sesame oil | 3 tablespoons toasted sesame seeds |

1. Preheat the oven to 425°F.

2. In the skillet, toss the asparagus with the olive oil. Season with salt and pepper. Sprinkle the garlic on top of the asparagus.

3. Transfer to the oven and roast until tender, 12 to 15 minutes.

4. In a small bowl, whisk together the sesame oil, tahini, lemon juice, warm water, and garlic powder.

5. Drizzle the tahini sauce over the asparagus, sprinkle with the toasted sesame seeds, and serve.

**INGREDIENT TIP:** Tahini is a paste made from sesame seeds that has a consistency similar to peanut butter. It is easily found at most grocery stores. If it's not with the nut butters, check the ethnic foods section.

# LEMON-PARMESAN FRIED CAULIFLOWER

**12" SKILLET** / One Pan / Quick & Easy / Vegetarian

**Serves 8 / Prep time: 10 minutes / Cook time: 10 minutes**

The first time I ever had fried cauliflower, my mother-in-law made it for me. I loved it so much that on a recent Christmas, when she asked me to pick something special for her to make, I chose her cauliflower. I helped her in the kitchen all Christmas day, and as it got later, no cauliflower was in sight. "Sheila . . . are you making my cauliflower?" I asked. She answered that she was, but could I just start by cutting the cauliflower. Next, she asked if I could make the bread crumb mixture. Then I should probably get the oil heated. You know where this is going. I ended up making my own fried cauliflower! Like all good cooks, Sheila is very good at delegating. But at least I learned how to make it.

| | |
|---|---|
| Vegetable oil, for frying | ½ teaspoon salt |
| ¾ cup all-purpose flour | ¼ teaspoon freshly ground black pepper |
| 2 large eggs, beaten | ¼ teaspoon ground cayenne pepper |
| 1 cup panko bread crumbs | 1 medium cauliflower head, cut into |
| ⅓ cup grated Parmesan cheese | medium florets |
| 1 tablespoon grated lemon zest | Lemon wedges, for serving |

1. Preheat the skillet over medium heat with an inch or two of vegetable oil.

2. Place the flour in one small bowl and the eggs in another. In a third small bowl, whisk together the bread crumbs, Parmesan cheese, lemon zest, salt, pepper, and cayenne.

3. Coat each cauliflower floret in the flour, then the egg, and then the bread crumb mixture.

4. Working in batches, carefully place a few of the coated florets in the hot oil and fry, turning to evenly cook all sides, until the cauliflower is tender and golden brown, about 5 minutes. Repeat with the remaining florets.

5. Place the fried cauliflower on paper towels, and season with salt. Serve immediately with lemon wedges.

**SERVING TIP:** I like this cauliflower simply served with a squeeze of fresh lemon, but it's also delicious with a garlic aioli.

# MEXICAN ELOTES CREAMED CORN

**12" SKILLET** / One Pan / Quick & Easy / Vegetarian

**Serves 4 / Prep time: 5 minutes / Cook time: 10 minutes**

Elotes is a classic Mexican street food. Grilled corn is smothered in mayo, crema, garlic, chili powder, and Cotija cheese. This dish is creamed corn meets elotes, and it's my husband's favorite. Best of all, this spicy, sweet, creamy, and unique side dish comes together in just a few minutes.

2 tablespoons unsalted butter

2 garlic cloves, minced

1 jalapeño pepper, seeded and thinly sliced

1 tablespoon all-purpose flour

½ cup whole milk

½ cup heavy (whipping) cream

1 pound fresh or frozen (thawed) corn kernels (about 4 cups)

2 teaspoons sugar

½ teaspoon chili powder

¼ teaspoon ground cumin

¼ teaspoon paprika

Salt

Freshly ground black pepper

¼ cup grated Parmesan cheese

¼ cup chopped fresh cilantro

⅓ cup crumbled Cotija cheese

1 lime, cut into 4 wedges

1. Preheat the skillet over medium heat. Melt the butter, then stir in the garlic and jalapeño pepper, and cook until softened, about 2 minutes.

2. Sprinkle the flour on top and stir, cooking the mixture for another minute. Slowly pour in the milk and cream, whisking constantly to avoid lumps. Add the corn.

3. Stir in the sugar, chili powder, cumin, and paprika. Season with salt and pepper. Let the mixture come to a low simmer, then cook, stirring often, until the sauce is thickened and the corn is tender, about 5 minutes.

4. Stir in the Parmesan cheese, and top with the fresh cilantro and Cotija cheese. Serve with lime wedges.

**INGREDIENT TIP:** This recipe is an especially delicious way to repurpose leftover grilled corn, which adds a great smoky flavor to this dish.

# SKILLET BAKED BEANS

**12" SKILLET** / One Pan / Weeknight

**Serves 4 to 6 / Prep time: 10 minutes / Cook time: 45 minutes**

Whether you're making them at home or over a campfire, baked beans are a crowd favorite. These skillet baked beans take a shortcut by using canned beans so they come together in half the time. But they don't sacrifice flavor. The additions of bacon, garlic, maple syrup, tomato paste, and liquid smoke build layers of sweet, savory, smoky flavor.

4 bacon slices, diced

½ yellow onion, diced

1 green bell pepper, diced

2 garlic cloves, minced

3 tablespoons tomato paste

3 tablespoons maple syrup

3 tablespoons brown sugar

1 tablespoon Worcestershire sauce

2 teaspoons apple cider vinegar

1 teaspoon Dijon mustard

¼ cup chicken broth

½ teaspoon smoked paprika

¼ teaspoon liquid smoke (optional)

1 (15-ounce) can pinto or navy beans, drained and rinsed

1 (15-ounce) can red kidney beans, drained and rinsed

Salt

Freshly ground black pepper

1.  Preheat the oven to 325°F, and preheat the skillet over medium heat.

2.  Cook the bacon until crispy, 6 to 8 minutes. Transfer the bacon to a paper towel–lined plate. Add the onion, bell pepper, and garlic to the pan with the bacon fat and cook until tender, 5 to 7 minutes.

3.  Stir in the tomato paste, maple syrup, brown sugar, Worcestershire, apple cider vinegar, and Dijon. Stir until combined, then add the broth, paprika, liquid smoke (if using), and beans. Stir in the bacon, and season with salt and pepper.

4.  Let the mixture come to a simmer, then transfer to the oven. Bake until the sauce is thick and sticky and the edges are slightly caramelized, about 30 minutes. Serve hot.

**SUBSTITUTION TIP:** To make this dish vegan, replace the chicken broth with vegetable stock or water and leave out the Worcestershire sauce and bacon. Use 2 tablespoons of olive oil in place of the bacon fat.

# PROVENÇAL HEIRLOOM TOMATOES

**12" SKILLET** / One Pan / Quick & Easy / Vegetarian

**Serves 4 / Prep time: 5 minutes / Cook time: 20 minutes**

Provençal tomatoes are traditionally whole tomatoes stuffed with bread crumbs, herbs, and cheese. Here, I like to use heirloom tomatoes (which also give this dish more color) and slice them instead of filling them whole. The tomatoes are layered in a skillet, topped with the bread crumb mixture, and baked until golden brown and bubbling. This recipe makes for a lovely side or light lunch when paired with a salad. Make sure to use perfectly ripe, in-season tomatoes here, as they are the real stars of this dish.

4 large, ripe heirloom tomatoes, sliced ½ inch thick

2 tablespoons extra-virgin olive oil, divided

Salt

Freshly ground black pepper

2 garlic cloves, minced

¾ cup fresh bread crumbs

⅓ cup grated Gruyère cheese

¼ cup grated Parmesan cheese

1 teaspoon herbes de Provence

¼ cup chopped fresh parsley

1. Preheat the oven to 425°F.

2. In the skillet, arrange the sliced tomatoes in slightly overlapping concentric circles. Drizzle with 1 tablespoon of olive oil, and season with salt and pepper. Sprinkle on the garlic.

3. In a small bowl, mix together the fresh bread crumbs, Gruyère and Parmesan cheeses, and herbes de Provence.

4. Sprinkle the bread crumb mixture evenly over top of the tomatoes, and season with additional salt and pepper. Drizzle with the remaining tablespoon of olive oil.

5. Bake the tomatoes until golden brown, 15 to 20 minutes. Top with the chopped parsley before serving.

**INGREDIENT TIP:** To make fresh bread crumbs, pulse day-old country bread (crusts removed) in a food processor to fine crumbs and season with salt and pepper. If you don't want to use fresh bread crumbs here, substitute with panko or plain, dry bread crumbs.

# MINI BUFFALO HASSELBACK POTATOES

**12″ SKILLET** / Gluten-Free / Grain-Free / One Pan / Vegetarian / Weeknight

Serves 4 / Prep time: 10 minutes / Cook time: 40 minutes

If you're not familiar with hasselback potatoes, they are the fanned and partly thinly sliced baked potatoes you see all over Pinterest nowadays. But these potatoes have actually been around since the 1950s, when they were first served at the Hasselbacken restaurant in Sweden. I like to give mine a spicy spin, glazed with a quick buffalo sauce and drizzled with a simple, homemade blue cheese dressing.

8 small gold potatoes

Extra-virgin olive oil, for drizzling

Salt

Freshly ground black pepper

4 tablespoons (½ stick) unsalted butter, melted

5 tablespoons hot sauce

⅓ cup crumbled blue cheese

½ cup whole-fat sour cream

¼ cup buttermilk

3 teaspoons freshly squeezed lemon juice

¼ cup chopped scallions, green parts only

1. Preheat the oven to 400°F.

2. Working from the top down, make thin cuts in each potato, ensuring you don't cut all the way through them, hasselback-style.

3. Drizzle the potatoes with olive oil, and season with salt and pepper. Place the potatoes in the skillet, cut-side up, and transfer to the oven. Bake for 35 minutes or until the potatoes are golden and tender.

4. In a small bowl, combine the melted butter and hot sauce. Brush this mixture evenly over the potatoes, and return them to the oven for 5 minutes. Remove from the oven.

5. In a medium bowl, whisk together the blue cheese, sour cream, buttermilk, and lemon juice, and season with salt and pepper. Drizzle the potatoes with the blue cheese dressing, garnish with the scallions, and serve.

**VARIATION TIP:** You can make these mini hasselback potatoes in various combinations and flavors using the same basic preparation. Try loaded-style, with Cheddar cheese, bacon, sour cream, and chives, or an herb and garlic version topped with lemon and nutty Parmesan cheese.

# MARSALA-GLAZED MUSHROOMS

**12" SKILLET** / Gluten-Free / One Pan / Quick & Easy / Vegetarian

**Serves 4 / Prep time: 10 minutes / Cook time: 10 minutes**

Being married to a mushroom hater is hard when you're a mushroom lover. If I make anything with mushrooms in it, I usually have to chop them large enough so that my husband can pick them out. But one exception to the rule is that he really likes chicken Marsala. These mushrooms take on all of the rich, luscious flavors of a great Marsala sauce and are my favorite mushroom side dish—ever.

2 tablespoons extra-virgin olive oil

1 pound cremini mushrooms, thickly sliced

1 shallot, diced

1 garlic clove, minced

Salt

Freshly ground black pepper

⅓ cup Marsala wine

2 tablespoons unsalted butter

2 teaspoons chopped fresh thyme

1. Preheat the skillet over medium heat. Heat the olive oil, add the mushrooms, and cook until softened, about 5 minutes.

2. Add the shallot and garlic to the pan, and season with salt and pepper. Continue cooking until the mixture has softened and browned and all of the liquid from the mushrooms has evaporated, another 5 to 7 minutes.

3. Deglaze the pan with the Marsala, using a wooden spoon to scrape up the browned bits from the bottom, and cook for another minute or so. Remove the pan from the heat and stir in the butter until it is fully melted. Stir in the thyme and serve.

**SUBSTITUTION TIP:** Make this side dish vegan by just leaving out the butter (it's still delicious without it) or stirring in a vegan butter at the end.

# ROASTED BUTTERNUT SQUASH WITH FETA AND POMEGRANATE

**14" SKILLET** / Gluten-Free / Grain-Free / One Pan / Vegetarian / Weeknight

**Serves 4 / Prep time: 10 minutes / Cook time: 30 minutes**

This recipe is a unique way to showcase this favorite winter squash. Pomegranate, also in peak season during fall and winter, pairs really well with butternut squash and feta, making this side sweet, fruity, savory, and tangy all in one bite. Not to mention: This might be the prettiest dish in this cookbook. The orange squash, flecks of scarlet pomegranate seeds, and bright green parsley look stunning, especially with cast iron as the canvas.

1 butternut squash, peeled, halved, seeded, and cut into ½-inch-thick slices

2 small shallots, peeled and quartered

2 tablespoons extra-virgin olive oil

1 tablespoon honey

Salt

Freshly ground black pepper

½ cup crumbled feta cheese

¼ cup pomegranate seeds

¼ cup chopped fresh parsley

1. Preheat the oven to 425°F.

2. In the skillet, combine the butternut squash and shallots with the olive oil and honey. Toss very well to coat, and season with salt and pepper.

3. Transfer to the oven and roast until caramelized and tender, 25 to 30 minutes, stirring halfway through.

4. Top the roasted squash with the feta cheese, pomegranate seeds, and parsley before serving.

**COOKING TIP:** Sliced squash makes for a more elegant presentation here, but you can certainly cut your squash into large cubes if you prefer. Many grocery stores sell fresh butternut squash that is already peeled, seeded, and cut for convenience.

# SZECHUAN GREEN BEANS

**12" SKILLET** / Gluten-Free / One Pan / Quick & Easy / Vegetarian

**Serves 4 / Prep time: 5 minutes / Cook time: 15 minutes**

One of my favorite places to eat in my town is this teeny-tiny Szechuan café. The restaurant is small but the flavors are big, and everything I eat there is always amazing. I am obsessed with a green bean dish on their menu called Sha Cha Green Beans, which features green beans, peanuts, and a Chinese barbecue sauce. It's smoky, slightly sweet, spicy, and delicious. This recipe is inspired by that dish and makes a great side, but it can also serve as a quick and easy vegetarian dinner paired with rice or tofu.

2 tablespoons vegetable oil

1 pound green beans, trimmed

2 teaspoons sambal oelek
  chili-garlic paste

3 tablespoons low-sodium soy sauce
  (see tip)

2 tablespoons hoisin sauce (see tip)

2 tablespoons rice vinegar

1 teaspoon sesame oil

3 garlic cloves, minced

3 teaspoons grated fresh ginger

¼ cup chopped toasted peanuts

1. Preheat the skillet over medium-high heat, and add the vegetable oil.

2. Add the green beans to the very hot skillet and fry, turning often, until they are shriveled, browned, and crisp-tender, 7 to 10 minutes.

3. In a small bowl, whisk together the chili-garlic paste, soy sauce, hoisin sauce, rice vinegar, sesame oil, garlic, and ginger. Pour the sauce over the green beans, and stir until the green beans are evenly coated and the sauce is bubbling and thick, 2 to 3 minutes.

4. Sprinkle the chopped peanuts on top and serve.

**SUBSTITUTION TIP:** To make this dish gluten-free, make sure to buy gluten-free soy sauce and hoisin sauce. Popular, commonly found brands such as Kikkoman offer both options.

# GRILLED HALLOUMI AND WATERMELON SKEWERS

**GRILL PAN** / Gluten-Free / Grain-Free / One Pan / Vegetarian

**Serves 8 / Prep time: 10 minutes / Cook time: 10 minutes**

Grilled watermelon is one of my absolute favorite summer staples, in both sweet and savory preparations. I love to grill it with halloumi cheese, which makes for especially fun and colorful skewers paired with fresh mint. Halloumi cheese becomes lightly charred and savory, while watermelon develops a deeper, smoky sweetness. The olives add briny saltiness, while mint and lime perk things up with a punch of acidity.

3 tablespoons extra-virgin olive oil, plus more for greasing

1 pound halloumi cheese, cut into 1-inch cubes

1 small seedless ripe watermelon, cut into 1-inch cubes

1 lime, zested and juiced

¼ cup chopped fresh mint

¼ cup chopped fresh parsley

½ cup pitted, chopped mixed Greek olives

Freshly ground black pepper

1. Heat the grill pan over medium heat, and grease it lightly with oil.

2. Thread the halloumi and watermelon cubes onto 8 wooden skewers.

3. Grill the skewers until the halloumi and watermelon are charred, 1 to 2 minutes per side.

4. In a small bowl, mix together the olive oil, lime juice, and lime zest. Stir in the mint, parsley, and olives.

5. Pour the olive mixture over the skewers, season with pepper, and serve warm.

**INGREDIENT TIP:** Halloumi is a firm white cheese made from a blend of goat's and sheep's milk with a savory, salty flavor profile. This cheese takes very well to being grilled or heated, as it retains its shape because of its high melting point.

# CARAMELIZED BROCCOLI WITH PINE NUTS AND PARMESAN

**12″ SKILLET** / Gluten-Free / Grain-Free / One Pan / Quick & Easy / Vegetarian

**Serves 2 to 4 / Prep time: 5 minutes / Cook time: 15 minutes**

When I was in culinary school in New York City, my mom would meet me after class on weekends and we'd go out for dinner. We loved trying new restaurants, but one of our favorites was a charming little old-world Italian spot. They had a charred broccolini dish on their appetizer menu that we adored, and this recipe reminds me of it. Nothing caramelizes vegetables quite like a cast iron skillet, which gives broccoli a sweeter, more complex flavor that is perfectly complemented by nutty Parmesan cheese and pine nuts.

2 tablespoons extra-virgin olive oil

1 head broccoli, trimmed and cut into spears

Salt

Freshly ground black pepper

¼ cup chicken or vegetable stock

2 garlic cloves, thinly sliced

¼ cup toasted pine nuts

⅓ cup grated Parmesan cheese

2 tablespoons freshly squeezed lemon juice

1.  Heat the skillet over medium heat until hot, then add the olive oil. Add the broccoli in an even layer and cook until it begins to brown and caramelize on the bottom, 5 to 7 minutes.

2.  Turn the broccoli over and continue cooking until slightly caramelized on the other side, another 3 to 4 minutes.

3.  Season with salt and pepper and deglaze the pan with the stock, using a wooden spoon to scrape up the browned bits from the bottom. Add the garlic and stir, cooking until the broccoli is tender and the broth has evaporated, another 3 minutes or so.

4.  Once the broccoli is caramelized and tender, add the pine nuts, Parmesan cheese, and lemon juice. Gently toss to combine before serving.

**SUBSTITUTION TIP:** If you don't have pine nuts around, walnuts are a delicious substitute for this dish.

*Beer-Battered Zucchini Tacos
with Avocado Crema
page 84*

# chapter five

# VEGETARIAN & VEGAN MAINS

# ONE-POT CAPRESE MACARONI AND CHEESE

**LARGE SKILLET OR MEDIUM DUTCH OVEN** / One Pan / Quick & Easy / Vegetarian

Serves 4 / Prep time: 10 minutes / Cook time: 10 minutes

I am so glad that one-pot macaroni and cheese is a thing. And what a glorious thing it is. If you've never made it before, it goes like this: Pasta gets cooked in milk until thick and creamy before the cheese gets stirred in. There's no draining, no dirtying several dishes, and the starch helps make a luscious sauce without the need for a roux. So easy, right? And delicious every time. I like making this caprese version, which features freshly grated mozzarella cheese, ripe tomatoes, and fresh basil.

8 ounces dry elbow pasta

2 cups whole milk

1 cup water

½ teaspoon salt

1 cup freshly grated mozzarella cheese

½ cup grated Parmesan cheese

2 tablespoons unsalted butter

¼ cup chopped fresh basil

1 cup seeded and diced ripe
  fresh tomato

Freshly ground black pepper

1.  Preheat the skillet or Dutch oven over medium heat. Add the pasta, milk, water, and salt. Bring the mixture to a simmer, stirring frequently to prevent the pasta from sticking.

2.  Let the pasta simmer until al dente, 8 to 10 minutes. The pasta will absorb most of the liquid, and the sauce will be thick and creamy.

3.  Remove from the heat and stir in the mozzarella cheese, a little at a time, until incorporated. Stir in the Parmesan cheese, butter, basil, and tomato. Season with pepper and serve immediately.

**INGREDIENT TIP:** Freshly grated cheese is a must for making macaroni and cheese. Prepackaged shredded cheeses contain anti-clumping additions, like cellulose, which keep the cheeses from melting properly. The result is lumpy sauce.

# MEDITERRANEAN QUESADILLAS

**12″ SKILLET** / One Pan / Quick & Easy / Vegetarian

**Serves 1 to 2 / Prep time: 10 minutes / Cook time: 5 minutes**

I love making quesadillas for many reasons. First, they're incredibly easy and can be ready in just 15 minutes, making them the perfect dinner after a hard day at work. Second, they're great to customize and have fun with. And last but not least, they come out amazing every single time in my trusty cast iron skillet. Here, I combine my favorite Mediterranean flavors; creamy hummus, salty feta, roasted red peppers, olives, and spinach make for a satisfying and unique meatless quesadilla.

2 (10-inch) flour tortillas

2 teaspoons extra-virgin olive oil

2 tablespoons hummus

¼ cup chopped baby spinach

1 tablespoon diced roasted red peppers

1 tablespoon diced red onion

1 tablespoon chopped kalamata olives

1 tablespoon crumbled feta cheese with Mediterranean herbs

1 tablespoon chopped fresh parsley

Tzatziki, for serving (optional)

1. Preheat the skillet over medium heat.

2. Brush the outside of both tortillas with the olive oil.

3. Spread 1 tablespoon of hummus on the inside of each tortilla. Top 1 tortilla evenly with the spinach, roasted peppers, onion, and olives. Sprinkle with the feta and parsley and top with the second tortilla.

4. Cook the quesadilla until evenly browned, golden, and hot, about 2 minutes per side.

5. Slice the quesadilla into 4 wedges and serve with tzatziki, if desired.

**SUBSTITUTION TIP:** Easily make this recipe vegan by using vegan tortillas (like Mission brand) and leaving out the feta cheese. You don't really need the cheese in this recipe: Hummus acts as the "glue."

# CHEESE PUPUSAS WITH CURTIDO

**12″ SKILLET OR GRIDDLE** / Gluten-Free / One Pan / Vegetarian

**Serves 4 / Prep time: 25 minutes, plus 24 hours to chill / Cook time: 20 minutes**

I'd never even heard of a pupusa until I met my husband. Ryan is half Honduran, and every holiday we've celebrated at his family's house has included pupusas. Although they are from El Salvador, they're also a popular street food in the neighboring Honduras. These plump, cheese-filled rounds are made from a thick, hand-formed masa cake—which also makes them gluten-free. Pupusas are traditionally served with curtido, a pickled cabbage slaw with a little bit of heat.

**FOR THE CURTIDO**

2 cups shredded green and purple cabbage

1 large carrot, peeled and grated

4 radishes, thinly sliced

½ jalapeño pepper, sliced

1 cup white vinegar

¼ cup water

½ teaspoon salt

1 teaspoon brown sugar

Pinch red pepper flakes

1 teaspoon dried oregano, plus
   more for serving

**FOR THE PUPUSAS**

2 cups masa harina, such as Maseca

1½ to 2 cups warm water, plus
   more if needed

½ cup finely grated queso fresco

½ teaspoon salt

Extra-virgin olive oil, for greasing

1 cup shredded mozzarella cheese

**TO MAKE THE CURTIDO** (Prepare at least 24 hours before serving the pupusas)

1.  In a large bowl, combine the cabbage, carrot, radishes, and jalapeño pepper.

2.  In a small microwavable bowl in the microwave or in a small saucepan over medium heat, heat the vinegar, water, salt, and brown sugar until the sugar is melted. Cool the mixture slightly, and pour it over the vegetables. Add the red pepper flakes and oregano and stir thoroughly.

3.  Transfer the curtido to an airtight container and place it in the refrigerator. The top of the cabbage mixture should be submerged in the liquid.

### TO MAKE THE PUPUSAS

1. In a large bowl, mix together the masa harina, warm water, queso fresco, and salt to form a soft dough. Start with 1½ cups of warm water. If the dough is too dry, add more water, tablespoon by tablespoon. The dough should be soft but not sticky, and should not crack when you form it into a ball.

2. When you get the right consistency, knead the dough for 1 minute, then cover with a clean, damp towel. Let rest for 15 minutes. Preheat the skillet or griddle over medium heat.

3. Divide the pupusa dough into 8 balls. Grease your hands with a little bit of oil, and form the dough into balls. Pat out each ball to form a disc. Place a few tablespoons of shredded mozzarella cheese in the center of each disc, and carefully pinch the dough around the cheese to form a rough ball again. Then, flatten each piece of dough into the final disc, about 4 inches wide.

4. Store the pupusas under a damp cloth to keep them moist.

5. Lightly grease the pan with oil (not too much) and cook the pupusas for 4 to 5 minutes per side, until they are charred in spots. Work in batches to avoid crowding.

6. Serve hot with the curtido and a pinch of oregano.

**VARIATION TIP:** Pupusas can be filled or topped with anything you'd like. Try refried beans, carnitas, shredded chicken, beef, or a combination of any of the above.

# KUNG PAO CAULIFLOWER

**12″ SKILLET OR WOK** / Gluten-Free / Quick & Easy / Vegan

**Serves 4 / Prep time: 10 minutes / Cook time: 20 minutes**

When I'm craving Chinese takeout, I like to make this healthier, vegan version of Kung Pao at home. This recipe uses two ingredients you may not be familiar with— sambal oelek, a spicy chili paste, and lemony Szechuan pepper. Both can be found at your local supermarket and make a world of difference in this Kung Pao sauce. These ingredients are also what make this dish spicy, so feel free to alter the heat to your taste.

**FOR THE CAULIFLOWER**

2 tablespoons vegetable oil, divided

1 medium head cauliflower, cut
   into florets

Salt

Freshly ground black pepper

1 green bell pepper, cut into thin strips

1 red bell pepper, cut into thin strips

1 large shallot, thinly sliced

2 garlic cloves, minced

**FOR THE SAUCE**

⅓ cup low-sodium soy sauce
   (gluten-free if needed)

1 tablespoon rice vinegar

1 tablespoon sambal oelek

1 tablespoon sesame oil

2 tablespoons brown sugar

½ teaspoon ground Szechuan pepper

2 teaspoons grated fresh ginger

3 teaspoons cornstarch

¼ cup vegetable stock

**FOR SERVING**

4 scallions, green parts only, chopped

¼ cup chopped peanuts

### TO MAKE THE CAULIFLOWER

1. Heat the skillet or wok over medium-high heat. Add 1 tablespoon of vegetable oil, and arrange the cauliflower in one even layer. Work in batches, if necessary, to avoid crowding the pan.

2. Cook the cauliflower, stirring occasionally, until golden brown and crisp-tender, 7 to 8 minutes. Season with salt and pepper. Remove the cauliflower from the skillet; set aside.

3. Add the remaining tablespoon of oil and cook the bell peppers and shallot until crisp-tender, about 3 minutes. Stir in the garlic and cook until fragrant, about 2 minutes.

### TO MAKE THE SAUCE

1. Meanwhile, in a small bowl, combine the soy sauce, rice vinegar, sambal oelek, sesame oil, brown sugar, Szechuan pepper, and fresh ginger. In another small bowl, stir the cornstarch into the vegetable stock until it is completely dissolved. Add this mixture to the sauce and whisk until incorporated.

2. Pour the sauce into the pan with the peppers and simmer until thickened, about 2 minutes. Add the cauliflower, and toss everything to evenly coat with the sauce.

### TO SERVE

Serve with the chopped scallions and peanuts on top.

**INGREDIENT TIP:** Sambal oelek is a spicy paste made from chili peppers, vinegar, and salt. It's found in the Asian foods aisle of most supermarkets

# BEER-BATTERED ZUCCHINI TACOS WITH AVOCADO CREMA

**12″ SKILLET** / One Pan / Vegetarian / Weeknight

**Serves 6 to 8 / Prep time: 15 minutes / Cook time: 20 minutes**

Living in San Diego for several years made me absolutely obsessed with fish tacos. This vegetarian version has become a favorite in my house. Zucchini gets coated in Mexican beer batter and fried until golden and crispy. Paired with a spicy and tangy slaw and creamy avocado-yogurt sauce, this dish is the star of any vegetarian taco night.

## FOR THE CREMA

1 ripe avocado, pitted and peeled

1 cup plain, whole-fat Greek yogurt

¼ cup roughly chopped fresh cilantro

Juice of 1 lime

½ teaspoon salt

Freshly ground black pepper

## FOR THE SLAW

2 cups shredded carrots

1 jalapeño pepper, sliced

1 teaspoon avocado oil or extra-virgin olive oil

1 tablespoon freshly squeezed lime juice

1 teaspoon sugar

½ teaspoon ground cumin

Salt

Freshly ground black pepper

½ cup chopped fresh cilantro

## FOR THE ZUCCHINI AND THE TACOS

Vegetable oil, for frying

1½ cups all-purpose flour, divided

1½ teaspoons baking powder

¼ teaspoon ground cayenne pepper

¼ teaspoon ground cumin

¼ teaspoon smoked paprika

1 teaspoon salt

Freshly ground black pepper

1 cup cold Mexican beer, like Corona

2 large zucchini

16 small corn tortillas

### TO MAKE THE CREMA

In a blender or food processor, blend the avocado, yogurt, cilantro, and lime juice until smooth. Season with the salt and pepper, and refrigerate until ready to use.

### TO MAKE THE SLAW

In a medium bowl, combine the carrots, jalapeño pepper, avocado oil, lime juice, sugar, and cumin, and season with salt and pepper. Toss thoroughly. Refrigerate until ready to use, and toss in the cilantro right before serving.

### TO MAKE THE ZUCCHINI AND THE TACOS

1. In the skillet over medium heat, heat 1 inch of vegetable oil until it reaches 350 to 375°F.

2. In a medium bowl, whisk to combine 1 cup of flour with the baking powder, cayenne, cumin, paprika, and salt, and season with black pepper. Pour in the beer, mix until combined, and let rest for 10 minutes. It should be the consistency of a thick pancake batter.

3. Slice the zucchini in half lengthwise, and cut each half in half again lengthwise. Cut each wedge in half so you have a total of 8 thick zucchini sticks.

4. Put the remaining ½ cup of flour in a shallow bowl. Toss each piece of zucchini in the flour, then coat in the beer batter. Working in batches, drop the coated zucchini into the hot skillet and fry until tender and evenly brown and golden on each side, about 2 minutes per side. Drain well on a paper towel–lined plate.

5. Wrap the corn tortillas in a damp paper towel and heat in the microwave for 30 seconds to 1 minute, until warm. Fill with the fried zucchini, crema, and slaw, and serve.

**SUBSTITUTION TIP:** To make this recipe gluten-free, use rice flour instead of all-purpose flour for the beer batter.

# CAULIFLOWER AND POTATO CURRY (ALOO GOBI)

**LARGE DUTCH OVEN** / Gluten-Free / Grain-Free / One Pan / Vegetarian / Weeknight

**Serves 6 to 8 / Prep time: 15 minutes / Cook time: 35 minutes**

This recipe will forever remind me of when I accidentally cut my finger so badly that I ended up in the ER. After seven hours in the emergency room and several stitches in my thumb, you'd think I'd never want to make this recipe again. But you'd be wrong. I still love this simple yet flavorful meatless Indian dish.

3 tablespoons extra-virgin olive oil or ghee

1 yellow onion, diced

1 teaspoon cumin seeds

1 small serrano pepper, minced

2 garlic cloves, minced

2 teaspoons grated fresh ginger

1 teaspoon ground turmeric

1½ teaspoons garam masala

¼ teaspoon paprika

Salt

Freshly ground black pepper

1 medium head cauliflower, cut into florets

3 russet potatoes, peeled and cut into cubes

1 (15-ounce) can crushed tomatoes

½ cup vegetable stock (or water)

½ cup peas, fresh or frozen

2 tablespoons unsalted butter

¼ cup chopped fresh cilantro

1. Preheat the Dutch oven over medium heat, and add olive oil. Add the onion and cook until softened and golden, about 7 minutes. Add the cumin seeds and cook for another minute.

2. Add the serrano pepper and garlic to the pot and cook until everything is soft and fragrant, about 3 minutes. Stir in the ginger, turmeric, garam masala, and paprika. Season with salt and pepper. Cook, stirring, for another minute, until the spices are fragrant. Stir in the cauliflower and potatoes, and toss to coat.

3. Stir in the crushed tomatoes and vegetable stock, and cook until simmering. Cover the Dutch oven and cook until the potatoes and cauliflower are tender but not falling apart, about 20 minutes.

4. Uncover the pot and add the peas and butter. Season with additional salt and pepper, if needed. Serve topped with the fresh cilantro.

**SERVING TIP:** Serve this dish over rice with raita (Indian yogurt-based condiment) or paired with Roasted Garlic Oil Naan (page 44).

# WHITE BEAN AND KALE CASSOULET

**12" SKILLET, SHEET PAN** / Vegetarian / Weeknight

**Serves 4 to 6 / Prep time: 15 minutes / Cook time: 45 minutes**

A cassoulet may sound fancy or difficult, but it's actually fairly simple. Cassoulets are French stews, typically made with meat and dried beans, which require overnight soaking and hours of slow simmering. Here, we take a shortcut with canned beans and substitute vegetables enhanced with wine, aromatics, and herbs. The addition of buttery, toasted bread makes this a hearty dish.

¼ cup extra-virgin olive oil

2 shallots, thinly sliced

1 leek, white and light green parts only, thinly sliced

3 garlic cloves, minced

1 parsnip, peeled and finely diced

2 carrots, peeled and finely diced

2 celery stalks, sliced

Salt

Freshly ground black pepper

¼ cup white wine

1 dried bay leaf

1 tablespoon chopped fresh rosemary

1 teaspoon chopped fresh thyme

Pinch ground cloves

2 (15-ounce) cans cannellini beans, drained but not rinsed

1 (15-ounce) can crushed tomatoes

1 cup vegetable stock

3 cups chopped kale

½ baguette, cut into medium cubes

3 tablespoons unsalted butter, melted

1. Preheat the oven to 375°F, and preheat the skillet over medium heat. Heat the olive oil, and add the shallots and leek. Sauté until the shallots and leek are softened and translucent, 5 to 7 minutes.

2. Stir in the garlic, parsnip, carrots, and celery. Season with salt and pepper and cook, stirring, until the vegetables are softened, about 8 minutes.

3. Deglaze the skillet with the wine, stirring up the browned bits from the bottom, and add the bay leaf, rosemary, thyme, and cloves. When the wine is nearly evaporated, after about 2 minutes, stir in the beans, crushed tomatoes, and stock. Stir to incorporate everything, and let simmer for 2 minutes. Add the kale and cook until wilted and tender, about 2 minutes.

4. Meanwhile, in a large bowl, toss the baguette with the melted butter. Transfer the coated bread cubes to a sheet pan and bake until lightly toasted, about 5 minutes.

5. Top the cassoulet with the bread cubes, pushing them down into the mixture so only the tops are sticking out a bit. Transfer the cassoulet to the oven and bake until the sauce is bubbling and the bread is golden, about 18 minutes. Serve warm.

**COOKING TIP:** If preferred, you can skip toasting the bread. Simply press the plain bread cubes into the cassoulet and drizzle with the butter. You may need to bake the cassoulet a bit longer to get the bread toasty and golden.

# LENTIL STEW WITH COLLARD GREENS AND SWEET POTATO

**LARGE DUTCH OVEN** / Gluten-Free / Grain-Free / One Pan / Vegan

Serves 6 to 8 / Prep time: 15 minutes / Cook time: 1 hour

Making a vegan meal that is comforting, rich, and satisfying can be challenging for me, because I'm so used to relying on butter and cheese when I'm craving comfort foods. However, this meal is 100% vegan and one I love to cozy up with in the dead of winter. Don't skimp on the olive oil here, and use the best quality you can find.

3 tablespoons extra-virgin olive oil, plus more for serving

1 medium yellow onion, diced

3 large carrots, diced

3 celery stalks, diced

4 garlic cloves, minced

1 (15-ounce) can fire-roasted tomatoes with juice

2 teaspoons ground cumin

1½ teaspoons ground turmeric

1 teaspoon curry powder

½ teaspoon dried oregano

½ teaspoon dried thyme

Pinch red pepper flakes

Salt

Freshly ground black pepper

4 cups vegetable stock

2 cups water

1 cup dry green lentils, rinsed

3 medium sweet potatoes, peeled and cubed

1 bunch collard greens, stems and ribs discarded, leaves cut into thin ribbons

Avocado slices, for serving

Lime wedges, for serving

1. Preheat the Dutch oven over medium heat. Heat 3 tablespoons of the olive oil.

2. Add the onion, carrots, celery, and garlic. Cook until softened but not browned, 7 to 10 minutes.

3. Add the fire-roasted tomatoes, along with the cumin, turmeric, curry powder, oregano, thyme, and red pepper flakes. Season with salt and pepper, and stir until combined.

4. Add the vegetable stock and water, and bring to a simmer. Once simmering, add the lentils. Cover and cook for 15 minutes.

5. Add the sweet potatoes and cook, covered, for 25 to 30 minutes, until the lentils and potatoes are tender. Add the collard greens just before the last 5 to 10 minutes of cooking. Add salt and pepper as needed.

6. Serve topped with avocado, fresh squeezed lime, and a drizzle of olive oil.

**COOKING TIP:** This stew tastes even better the next day. Gently reheat and thin it out with additional stock if the stew has thickened too much.

# CREAMY CACCIATORE POLENTA

**12″ SKILLET, MEDIUM DUTCH OVEN** / Gluten-Free / Vegetarian / Weeknight

**Serves 4 / Prep time: 5 minutes / Cook time: 35 minutes**

This is my absolute favorite way to eat polenta—creamy and buttery and topped with the components of a cacciatore dish, but without any meat. Grape tomatoes are blistered in cast iron and paired with kalamata olives, white wine, capers, roasted red peppers, and herbs. The cacciatore can be done as the polenta cooks, making this a quick and impressive meal.

3 cups water

¾ teaspoon salt, plus more for serving

¾ cup yellow cornmeal

½ cup grated Parmesan cheese, plus more for serving

2 tablespoons unsalted butter

1 tablespoon extra-virgin olive oil, plus more for serving

1 pound grape tomatoes

1 garlic clove, minced

¼ cup white wine

¼ cup vegetable stock

1 tablespoon capers

¼ cup chopped kalamata olives

½ cup thinly sliced roasted red peppers

¼ teaspoon crushed red pepper flakes

Freshly ground black pepper

2 tablespoons minced fresh basil

1. In a medium Dutch oven, bring the water and salt to a boil. Slowly whisk in the cornmeal (polenta), a little at a time, to avoid clumping. Reduce the heat to medium-low and cook the polenta, stirring often, until thick, tender, and creamy, about 20 minutes. Once the polenta is soft, remove the pot from the heat and stir in the Parmesan cheese and butter.

2. Meanwhile, preheat the skillet over medium heat. Heat the olive oil, then add the grape tomatoes and spread them out in one even layer. Stir the tomatoes once they begin to blister on the bottom, after about 5 minutes, and cook until they are softened, charred, and beginning to release their juices, about 5 minutes more.

3. Add the garlic and cook for another minute. Pour in the white wine and simmer until reduced, about 2 minutes. Add the vegetable stock.

4. Add in the capers, olives, roasted red peppers, and red pepper flakes. Season with salt and pepper.

5. Divide the polenta among 4 bowls, and spoon the cacciatore mixture on top. Garnish with a drizzle of olive oil, fresh basil, and grated Parmesan cheese, if desired.

**COOKING TIP:** To make this recipe easier, you can buy store-bought polenta, slice it into thick rounds, fry it in a hot skillet with olive oil until golden, and serve it topped with the cacciatore sauce.

# EGGPLANT PARMESAN RATATOUILLE

**12" SKILLET, MEDIUM DUTCH OVEN** / Vegetarian

**Serves 6 to 8 / Prep time: 25 minutes / Cook time: 1 hour**

This recipe combines ratatouille and eggplant Parmesan into one incredible and delicious way to use your Dutch oven. My best friend, Sara, is also a professional chef, and no one makes fried eggplant as good as she does. Her secrets include using panko seasoned with lemon zest and herbs and never skipping the three-part breading method. This yields perfectly golden and crisp fried eggplant, ideal for soaking up the sauce.

**FOR THE EGGPLANT**

Vegetable oil, for frying

½ cup all-purpose flour

2 large eggs, beaten

1½ cups panko bread crumbs

½ cup grated Parmesan cheese

1 teaspoon dried oregano

½ cup finely chopped fresh parsley

½ lemon, zested

1 large eggplant, peeled and sliced
  ½ inch thick

Salt

Freshly ground black pepper

**FOR THE RATATOUILLE**

2 tablespoons extra-virgin olive oil

1 onion, diced

2 garlic cloves, minced

1 red bell pepper, diced

1 green bell pepper, diced

2 zucchini, cubed

2 yellow squash, cubed

2 Roma tomatoes, seeded and diced

Salt

Freshly ground black pepper

3 cups quality tomato sauce, divided

1 dried bay leaf

¼ teaspoon dried thyme

¼ teaspoon dried oregano

¼ teaspoon crushed red pepper flakes

1 teaspoon freshly squeezed lemon juice

2 cups shredded mozzarella cheese,
  divided

¼ cup chopped fresh parsley or basil,
  for serving

### TO MAKE THE EGGLANT

1. Heat the skillet with enough vegetable oil to cover the bottom.

2. Set out two small bowls: one with flour and one with the beaten eggs. In a medium bowl, mix well to combine the panko, Parmesan cheese, oregano, parsley, and lemon zest.

3. Dip each piece of eggplant in the flour and shake off the excess, then dip it in the egg and finally in the bread crumb mixture.

4. Add the eggplant to the hot skillet in batches, taking care to not overcrowd the pan. Fry until golden brown, about 2 minutes per side. Drain on a paper towel-lined plate, and season lightly with salt and pepper while still hot.

### TO MAKE THE RATATOUILLE

1. Preheat the oven to 350°F. Preheat the Dutch oven over medium heat. Heat the olive oil until hot. Sauté the onion and garlic until softened but not browned, 5 to 7 minutes. Add the red pepper, green pepper, zucchini, yellow squash, and Roma tomatoes. Season with salt and pepper. Cook, stirring the mixture occasionally, until the vegetables are barely softened, about 5 minutes.

2. Add in 1 cup of tomato sauce and the bay leaf, thyme, oregano, and red pepper flakes. Simmer the ratatouille for 5 minutes. Stir in the lemon juice.

3. Add 1 cup of mozzarella cheese on top of the ratatouille. Layer the eggplant slices, slightly overlapping, on top of the mozzarella. Pour the remaining 2 cups of sauce on top of the eggplant. Top with the remaining cup of mozzarella.

4. Transfer to the oven and cook, uncovered, until the cheese is melted and everything is hot and bubbly, 30 to 35 minutes. Serve topped with the fresh parsley.

**INGREDIENT TIP:** You can use a store-bought tomato sauce here. I recommend a high-quality brand such as Rao's.

# MUSHROOM STOUT SHEPHERD'S PIE

**12" SKILLET, LARGE POT** / Vegetarian

Servings: 8 / Prep time: 10 minutes / Cook time: 1 hour, 5 minutes

My grandmother was Irish, so I grew up with shepherd's pie. My mom made a version of it at home, tailored to my vegetable-hating dad, which we just called "meat pie." You wouldn't find carrots, celery, or peas in my mom's meat pie, only mushrooms, which my dad could tolerate. Mushrooms have since become one of my favorite additions to shepherd's pie. I don't miss the meat at all in this earthy, rich vegetarian version.

2½ pounds gold potatoes, peeled and chopped

Salt

2 tablespoons extra-virgin olive oil

1 onion, diced

2 garlic cloves, minced

2 carrots, peeled and medium diced

2 celery stalks, diced

1 parsnip, peeled and medium diced

Freshly ground black pepper

1 pound cremini mushrooms, sliced

2 portobello mushroom caps, diced

2 tablespoons tomato paste

1 tablespoon vegetarian Worcestershire sauce

1 cup Irish stout beer, such as Guinness

½ cup vegetable stock

½ cup whole milk

6 tablespoons (¾ stick) unsalted butter

¼ cup cold water

1 tablespoon cornstarch

½ cup frozen peas

1 tablespoon minced fresh rosemary

1 teaspoon minced fresh thyme

1. In a large pot, cover the potatoes with cold water. Salt the water and bring to a boil. Cook until the potatoes are fork-tender, about 20 minutes.

2. Meanwhile, preheat the skillet over medium heat and heat the olive oil. Add the onion and garlic and cook until translucent, about 5 minutes. Add the carrots, celery, and parsnip and cook for 5 to 7 minutes more, until slightly softened. Season with salt and pepper.

3. Add the cremini and portobello mushrooms and continue cooking until they soften and release their moisture, about 8 minutes.

4. Stir in the tomato paste and Worcestershire sauce, cook for 1 minute, and then add the beer and vegetable stock. Deglaze the pan, scraping the browned bits off the bottom, and simmer until the liquid is reduced by about half, 10 to 15 minutes.

5. While the filling is simmering, drain the potatoes. In a microwave-safe mug in the microwave or in a small saucepan on the stove over medium heat, warm the milk and butter. Mash the potatoes slightly, add the warm butter-milk mixture, season with salt and pepper, and continue mashing until smooth.

6. Preheat the oven broiler to high.

7. In a small bowl, stir the cold water and cornstarch together to make a slurry. Stir the slurry, peas, rosemary, and thyme into the mushroom filling. Let it simmer for 2 minutes or so, until thickened. Taste your filling, and add more salt and pepper if necessary.

8. Top the filling with the mashed potatoes, spreading evenly. Place the entire cast iron pan in the oven under the preheated broiler. Heat until the potatoes are golden brown, 3 to 5 minutes, and serve.

**COOKING TIP:** You can use store-bought or leftover mashed potatoes here. You'll need roughly 4 cups of prepared mashed potatoes for this recipe.

# FALAFEL BURGERS WITH MINT YOGURT

**12" SKILLET** / One Pan / Vegetarian / Weeknight

**Serves 4 / Prep time: 15 minutes, plus 20 minutes to chill / Cook time: 15 minutes**

My friend Sara and I love falafels so much that during college, we would drive into Manhattan in the middle of the night for them. An hour drive might seem excessive for a $2 falafel sandwich, especially considering we paid a Lincoln Tunnel toll five times that, but we had a favorite spot in Greenwich Village, and nothing else would do. Most of the prep time for these falafel-meets-burger patties is hands-off, letting them chill between forming and frying. A cool, creamy mint yogurt crowns them, and they're great served either on sesame buns or stuffed into pitas.

## FOR THE MINT YOGURT

1 cup plain, whole-fat Greek yogurt

¼ cup finely chopped fresh mint leaves

1 tablespoon freshly squeezed
   lemon juice

2 teaspoons extra-virgin olive oil

Salt

Freshly ground black pepper

2 teaspoons water, if needed

## FOR THE BURGERS

1 (15-ounce) can chickpeas, drained,
   rinsed, and dried

½ red onion, coarsely chopped

1 small jalapeño pepper, seeded
   and chopped

3 garlic cloves

½ cup chopped fresh parsley

1 tablespoon freshly squeezed
   lemon juice

1 tablespoon tahini

2 teaspoons ground cumin

1½ teaspoons ground coriander

¾ teaspoon salt

½ teaspoon freshly ground black pepper

¼ cup all-purpose flour

1 large egg white

⅓ cup panko bread crumbs

About 2 tablespoons vegetable oil
   (enough to just coat the skillet),
   for frying

4 sesame seed burgers or pitas,
   for serving

½ cucumber, thinly sliced, for serving

1 Roma tomato, thinly sliced, for serving

### TO MAKE THE MINT YOGURT

In a medium bowl, stir together the yogurt, mint, lemon juice, and olive oil until incorporated. Season with salt and pepper. If needed, thin the yogurt with 1 to 2 teaspoons water. Refrigerate until ready to use.

### TO MAKE THE BURGERS

1. Preheat the oven to 350°F.

2. In a food processor, blend the chickpeas, red onion, jalapeño pepper, garlic, parsley, lemon juice, tahini, cumin, coriander, salt, and pepper until incorporated. The mixture should still have a little bit of texture.

3. Transfer the mixture to a large bowl, and stir in the flour and egg white.

4. Shape the falafel mixture into 4 equal-size patties. (Place the mixture in the refrigerator for a few minutes to firm up slightly, if needed.)

5. Pour the panko onto a plate or shallow dish. Press each patty into the panko, and turn to evenly coat all sides. Place the formed patties in the refrigerator for 20 minutes to firm up and allow the flavors to meld together.

6. Preheat the skillet over medium heat with the vegetable oil. Fry the patties until they are golden brown on the bottom, 3 to 5 minutes. Flip and cook on the other side for 2 minutes.

7. Transfer the cast iron pan to the oven to finish cooking the patties. Cook until golden and heated through, about 5 minutes.

8. Remove from the oven and let the patties rest for 3 minutes. Assemble your burgers using your bread of choice, and serve topped with the mint yogurt, cucumber, and tomato slices.

**STORAGE TIP:** If you have leftovers, place a piece of parchment paper between each patty and store them in an airtight plastic bag in the refrigerator or freezer. Reheat patties in the oven at 350°F until heated through.

# RISOTTO WITH MASCARPONE AND ASPARAGUS

**MEDIUM DUTCH OVEN, MEDIUM POT** / Gluten-Free / Vegetarian / Weeknight

**Serves 4 to 6 / Prep time: 10 minutes / Cook time: 30 minutes**

Risotto scares off a lot of people, but give it a shot and you'll find it's actually fairly simple and requires few ingredients. The success of risotto is in the process—yes, you do have to babysit it, but only for 20 minutes. When I worked as the pastry chef for an Italian restaurant, I was always so jealous of the prep cook who made the risotto. I love the process; I find it therapeutic and relaxing. Maybe you will, too.

2 tablespoons extra-virgin olive oil

2 tablespoons unsalted butter

5 cups vegetable stock (use chicken
  if not vegetarian)

1 shallot, finely diced

2 garlic cloves, minced

1½ cups Arborio rice

½ cup white wine

12 asparagus spears, trimmed

1 lemon, finely zested

½ cup mascarpone cheese

½ cup grated Parmesan cheese, plus
  more for serving

1.  Preheat a medium Dutch oven over medium heat with the olive oil and butter. In a medium pot, bring the vegetable stock to a simmer.

2.  Add the shallot and garlic to the Dutch oven and cook until translucent, about 5 minutes. Stir in the rice and cook for 2 minutes, until lightly toasted.

3.  Pour in the wine, and continue cooking until all of the wine is evaporated, about 2 minutes.

4. Slowly stir in the hot stock, 1 cup at a time. Let the rice absorb all of the liquid before adding more stock. Repeat this process until all of the liquid is added, the sauce is very creamy, and the rice is tender but still slightly al dente. This should take about 20 minutes.

5. While the risotto is cooking, boil a medium pot of water and blanch the asparagus until tender, 2 to 4 minutes, then immediately plunge it into a bowl of ice water. Cut the blanched asparagus on the bias into 1- to 2-inch pieces.

6. When the risotto is done, remove the pot from the heat and stir in the lemon zest, mascarpone, and Parmesan cheese. Mix until incorporated and creamy. Lastly, stir in the asparagus.

7. Serve topped with additional Parmesan cheese.

**VARIATION TIP:** Not a fan of asparagus? Add 8 ounces sautéed mushrooms or ½ cup blanched peas instead. This recipe is also delicious topped with sautéed scallops.

# SKILLET LASAGNA WITH ZUCCHINI, PESTO, AND GOAT CHEESE

**10" SKILLET, LARGE POT** / Vegetarian

Serves 6 to 8 / Prep time: 15 minutes / Cook time: 45 minutes, plus
10 minutes to cool

Growing up in my Italian family meant lasagna at least once a week and on every single holiday or special occasion, ever. I'm not complaining—lasagna is delicious, filling, and easy to make. I like this version in the summer, when my garden is full of basil and zucchini. You can make your own pesto (see tip) or use store-bought. Goat cheese replaces the traditional ricotta in this recipe for a slightly tangy spin.

12 lasagna noodles

Salt

3 tablespoons extra-virgin olive oil, divided, plus a splash for the noodles

1 shallot, minced

2 garlic cloves, minced

2 zucchini, halved lengthwise and sliced

Freshly ground black pepper

5 ounces baby spinach

8 ounces goat cheese, at room temperature

1/3 cup whole milk

1 large egg

1¼ cups basil pesto, divided, plus more for serving (see tip)

1/3 cup grated Parmesan cheese

8 ounces shredded mozzarella cheese

1. Preheat the oven to 375°F, and preheat the skillet over medium heat.

2. Bring a large pot of salted water to a boil, and cook the lasagna noodles according to package directions until al dente. Drain and toss with a splash of olive oil to prevent sticking. When cooled, cut the noodles in half to yield 24 short lasagna noodles.

3. Meanwhile, in the skillet, heat 2 tablespoons of olive oil and sauté the shallot and garlic until softened, about 5 minutes. Add the zucchini and cook until nearly tender, about 5 minutes. Season with salt and pepper. Stir in the spinach and cook until wilted, about 3 minutes. Transfer the vegetable mixture to a large bowl.

4. In a medium bowl, mix the goat cheese with the milk and egg until smooth and creamy, the consistency of ricotta. Stir in ¼ cup of pesto, and season with salt and pepper.

5. Swirl the remaining tablespoon of oil around the cast iron skillet. Spread a bit of the pesto on the bottom of the pan, and layer on 6 lasagna noodles, slightly overlapping (4 across and 1 each on the top and bottom). Spread one-third of the goat cheese mixture on top. Layer one-third of the vegetable mixture on top of the goat cheese, and drizzle with one-quarter each of the remaining pesto and Parmesan cheese.

6. Repeat this process until you have 4 layers of noodles. Top with the last quarter of the pesto and the Parmesan cheese. Evenly sprinkle on all of the mozzarella cheese.

7. Transfer to the oven and bake, uncovered, until the sauce is bubbling and the cheese is golden brown at the edges, 25 to 30 minutes. Let cool for 10 minutes, then cut into 8 slices.

8. Serve topped with additional pesto, if desired.

**INGREDIENT TIP:** To make your own pesto, blend 2 cups packed fresh basil leaves, ⅓ cup grated Parmesan cheese, 2 ounces toasted pine nuts, and 4 garlic cloves in a food processor until finely chopped. With the processor running, slowly drizzle in ½ cup extra-virgin olive oil and season with salt and pepper.

# SWEET POTATO ENCHILADA SKILLET

**12" TO 14" SKILLET** / Gluten-Free / One Pan / Vegetarian / Weeknight

**Serves: 4 to 6 / Prep time: 10 minutes / Cook time: 30 minutes**

My friend Tricia, of Rhubarbarians.com, is the queen of vegetarian cooking and helped me test this recipe. Her first thought on the original recipe was that it needed more cheese, so it's obvious why we're friends. This is a delicious vegetable-laden weeknight meal, made quicker by eliminating the tedious process of individually filling each enchilada.

2 tablespoons extra-virgin olive oil

1 yellow onion, diced

1 jalapeño pepper, diced

3 garlic cloves, minced

2 cups peeled, finely diced sweet
   potatoes (about 1 large)

Salt

Freshly ground black pepper

¾ cup fresh or frozen corn

1 teaspoon ground cumin

½ teaspoon dried oregano

1 teaspoon chili powder

1 (15-ounce) can black beans, drained
   and rinsed

2 cups enchilada sauce (see tip)

6 small corn tortillas, torn or cut into
   strips (see tip)

2 cups grated Monterey Jack cheese

¼ cup chopped fresh cilantro

½ cup crumbled Cotija cheese

1 avocado, diced

Whole-fat sour cream, for serving

Lime wedges, for serving

*Quick Turmeric Seafood Paella*
*page 113*

1. Preheat the oven to 425°F, and preheat the skillet over medium heat.

2. Heat the olive oil. Add the onion and sauté until soft and lightly golden, 5 minutes. Stir in the jalapeño pepper, garlic, and sweet potatoes and cook, stirring frequently, until the potatoes are tender, about 10 minutes. Season with salt and pepper.

3. Stir in the corn, cumin, oregano, chili powder, black beans, and enchilada sauce. Bring the mixture to a simmer, and let it cook for 2 to 3 minutes.

4. Fold in the tortilla strips and ½ cup of Monterey Jack cheese. Sprinkle the top evenly with the remaining 1½ cups of Monterey Jack cheese, and transfer the skillet to the oven.

5. Bake until the sauce is bubbling and the cheese is melted, 10 to 12 minutes.

6. Top with the cilantro, Cotija cheese, and avocado, and serve with sour cream and lime wedges.

**INGREDIENT TIP:** This recipe is gluten-free; just ensure that you are using gluten-free corn tortillas and enchilada sauce, as some prepared enchilada sauces are made with flour. I recommend either 365 Organic or Frontera brands.

# chapter
# six
# FISH & POULTRY

# FENNEL, CITRUS, AND WHITE WINE SHRIMP

**12" SKILLET** / Gluten-Free / One Pan / Quick & Easy

Serves 2 to 4 / Prep time: 10 minutes / Cook time: 20 minutes

Fennel and fresh citrus is one of my favorite flavor combinations, especially when paired with seafood. This dish is light, sweet, and balanced. It makes a great dinner served over rice with asparagus. Feel free to experiment with different citrus here.

2 tablespoons extra-virgin olive oil, divided

1 pound raw tail-on shrimp, peeled and deveined

1 teaspoon sweet paprika

Salt

Freshly ground black pepper

1 shallot, thinly sliced

1 fennel bulb, halved, cored, and sliced

3 garlic cloves, minced

¼ cup white wine

3 tablespoons freshly squeezed lemon juice

3 tablespoons freshly squeezed orange juice

1 teaspoon grated lemon zest

1 teaspoon crushed fennel seeds

2 navel oranges, supremed (see tip)

1 tablespoon chopped fresh tarragon

1. Preheat the skillet over medium heat, then heat 1 tablespoon of olive oil. Season the shrimp on both sides with the paprika and salt and pepper. Add the shrimp to the hot skillet and cook until just pink, about 2 minutes per side.

2. Transfer the shrimp to a plate and set aside. Heat the remaining tablespoon of oil in the skillet, and add the shallot and fennel. Cook until golden and lightly caramelized, 5 to 10 minutes. Stir in the garlic and cook for another minute.

3. Deglaze the pan with the wine, using a wooden spoon to scrape up the browned bits from the bottom, and let it bubble for 1 to 2 minutes. Stir in the lemon juice, orange juice, lemon zest, fennel seeds, and oranges. Let the sauce simmer for 3 to 5 minutes, until slightly reduced and thickened. Taste and adjust seasonings.

4. Stir back in the cooked shrimp to warm it through. Serve garnished with the fresh tarragon.

**COOKING TIP:** To supreme an orange, slice off the top and bottom and stand the fruit up on its cut end for stability. Using a paring knife, carefully slice down the sides of the orange to remove the peel and pith, following the shape of the orange. Then, carefully slice out the orange segments in between the membranes.

# CREAMY COCONUT-SALMON CHOWDER

**MEDIUM DUTCH OVEN** / Gluten-Free / Grain-Free / One Pan / Weeknight

Serves 6 / Prep time: 10 minutes / Cook time: 30 minutes

This recipe is paleo and Whole30-compliant, which also makes it gluten-free and dairy-free. A chowder without dairy is certainly unorthodox, but I promise it works.

2 tablespoons extra-virgin olive oil, divided

3 ounces prosciutto, diced

1 leek, white and light green parts only, diced

1 cup peeled, diced carrots (about 3 medium)

1 cup diced celery (about 4 medium stalks)

Salt

Freshly ground black pepper

3 garlic cloves, minced

4 cups chicken bone broth

1½ pounds yellow potatoes, peeled and diced

1 lemon, zested and juiced, plus more for serving

1 dried bay leaf

20 ounces full-fat coconut milk (1½ cans)

1 pound wild-caught salmon, skinned and deboned

¼ cup chopped fresh parsley, plus more for serving

¼ cup chopped fresh dill, plus more for serving

Lemon wedges, for serving

1. Preheat the Dutch oven over medium heat with 1 tablespoon of olive oil, and cook the prosciutto until crisp and browned, 3 to 4 minutes. Transfer the prosciutto to a paper towel–lined plate and set aside.

2. In the same pot, heat the remaining tablespoon of olive oil and add the leek, carrots, and celery. Cook until the vegetables begin to soften and get a bit of color, 8 to 10 minutes. Season with salt and pepper. Add the garlic.

3. Add the chicken bone broth, potatoes, lemon zest and juice, and bay leaf. Bring to a simmer. Simmer until the potatoes are tender, about 15 minutes. Stir in the coconut milk.

4. Cut the salmon into 1-inch pieces and add it to the pot; simmer until the salmon is just cooked through and flaky, 3 to 4 minutes. Check the seasoning, adding salt and pepper if necessary.

5. Gently stir in the parsley and dill. Discard the bay leaf, and serve the chowder topped with the prosciutto, a sprinkling of additional herbs, and lemon wedges.

# PECAN-CRUSTED FISH WITH SWEET POTATO CHIPS

**10″ SKILLET** / Weeknight

**Serves 4 / Prep time: 20 minutes / Cook time: 30 minutes**

One rainy evening, after a particularly bad day at culinary school, I hopped on the subway and headed to my favorite fish-and-chips shop in Greenwich Village. I accidentally got off at the wrong stop, but I had an umbrella, so I decided to walk. Halfway there, a huge gust of wind turned my umbrella inside out and snapped it like a twig. I walked the rest of the way in the rain and stumbled into the fish-and-chips shop, soaking wet. No fish-and-chips have ever tasted better than those did, but this recipe comes close. These have a Southern spin with a crunchy pecan crust and quick and easy sweet potato "chips."

**FOR THE CHIPS**

1 pound sweet potatoes, peeled and cut into ¼-inch-thick sticks

2 tablespoons extra-virgin olive oil

1 tablespoon cornstarch

½ teaspoon paprika

½ teaspoon garlic powder

½ teaspoon salt

½ teaspoon freshly ground black pepper

**FOR THE FISH**

¾ cup all-purpose flour

¼ teaspoon cayenne pepper

½ teaspoon salt

½ teaspoon freshly ground black pepper

2 large eggs

¾ cup finely chopped toasted pecans

¾ cup plain bread crumbs

4 skinless halibut fillets

4 tablespoons oil

4 tablespoons (½ stick) unsalted butter

### TO MAKE THE CHIPS

1. Preheat the oven to 450°F.

2. In a large bowl of cold water, soak the sweet potatoes for 15 minutes. Drain and pat dry.

3. In a large bowl, toss the sweet potatoes with the olive oil until evenly coated. In a small bowl, mix together the cornstarch, paprika, garlic powder, salt, and pepper; toss to coat.

4. Spread the potatoes on a parchment-lined baking sheet in a single layer. Transfer to the oven and bake until golden and crispy, 25 to 30 minutes, flipping once halfway through. Remove from the oven, and season with salt while still hot.

### TO MAKE THE FISH

1. Preheat the skillet over medium heat.

2. Set out 3 small bowls. In the first bowl, whisk the flour with the cayenne, salt, and pepper. In the second bowl, whisk the eggs. In the third bowl, combine the pecans and bread crumbs.

3. Cut the halibut into equal-size (2- to 3-inch) pieces. Warm the oil and butter in the skillet until hot.

4. Coat each halibut piece in the flour, then dip it into the eggs. Lastly, coat the halibut in the pecan mixture.

5. Fry the halibut in two batches, making sure to not overcrowd the pan. Fry until the fish is golden brown on all sides and it flakes easily with a fork, 2 to 3 minutes per side. Serve with the sweet potato chips.

**COOKING TIP:** Cutting the halibut into even 2- to 3-inch pieces ensures a golden exterior and a flaky interior. Frying the fish in equal parts oil and butter imparts a lot of flavor to this dish, but it's important to not let the butter burn or smoke.

# SCALLOP PICCATA

**10″ SKILLET** / Gluten-Free / Grain-Free / One Pan / Quick & Easy

**Serves 2 / Prep time: 5 minutes / Cook time: 10 minutes**

When I need an elegant and delicious recipe that comes together in 15 minutes, start to finish, scallops are always my first choice. Scallops cook in a breeze and need only a simple sauce to let them shine. Here, I like to make a version of piccata—with garlic, lemon, white wine, and capers. This sauce creates the perfect balance of richness, acidity, and salt to complement the sweet scallops.

| | |
|---|---|
| 1 pound scallops | ½ cup dry white wine |
| Salt | 1 lemon, zested and juiced |
| Freshly ground black pepper | 2 tablespoons unsalted butter |
| 1 tablespoon extra-virgin olive oil | 2 tablespoons capers |
| 2 garlic cloves, minced | ¼ cup chopped fresh parsley, divided |

1. Preheat the skillet over medium heat. Pat the scallops dry, and season both sides with salt and pepper.

2. Heat the olive oil in the skillet, and cook the scallops until browned on each side, 1 to 2 minutes per side. Transfer to a plate.

3. Add the garlic to the skillet with the leftover oil and cook for a few seconds, until fragrant. Deglaze the pan with the wine, using a wooden spoon to scrape up the browned bits from the bottom.

4. Cook until the wine reduces by half, about 5 minutes, and remove from the heat. Stir in the lemon zest, lemon juice, and butter until smooth. Stir in the capers and about half of the parsley.

5. Return the scallops to the warm sauce and toss to coat. Top with the remaining fresh parsley and serve.

**SERVING TIP:** This recipe is delicious served with sautéed spinach or pasta.

**COOKING TIP:** Overcooked scallops are tough and chewy. To avoid this and cook scallops perfectly, ensure that your skillet is very hot. Scallops only need about 2 minutes per side to cook. They should look opaque all the way through and feel firm but still slightly soft to the touch.

# QUICK TURMERIC SEAFOOD PAELLA

**12" SKILLET** / Gluten-Free / One Pan / Weeknight

**Serves 6 / Prep time: 10 minutes / Cook time: 40 minutes**

While the idea of this recipe is to embody the culinary wonder that is paella, not emulate it, it doesn't stray far from the traditional dish. Mix up your protein with any combination of sausage, shrimp, mussels, chicken, calamari, scallops, or clams.

2 tablespoons extra-virgin olive oil, divided

11 ounces linguica sausage, sliced

1 pound raw shrimp, peeled and deveined

Salt

Freshly ground black pepper

1 yellow onion, diced

3 garlic cloves, minced

1 green bell pepper, diced

1 teaspoon ground turmeric

½ teaspoon smoked paprika

1 tablespoon tomato paste

8 ounces uncooked yellow Spanish rice, like Vigo

½ cup white wine

1¾ cups chicken stock

¾ cup peas

½ pound mussels

1. Preheat the skillet over medium heat. Heat 1 tablespoon of olive oil, and add the sausage. Cook until browned on both sides, about 4 minutes. Transfer to a plate and set aside.

2. Add the shrimp to the hot skillet and cook until just pink, about 2 minutes per side. Season with salt and pepper, and set aside with the sausage.

3. Add the remaining tablespoon of oil to the skillet, along with the onion, garlic, and bell pepper. Cook until the mixture is softened and golden, 5 to 7 minutes. Season with the turmeric and paprika, along with salt and pepper. Stir in the tomato paste and cook for another minute.

4. Stir in the yellow rice and toast for 1 to 2 minutes. Deglaze the pan with the wine, using a wooden spoon to scrape up any browned bits from the bottom. Add the chicken stock, and bring to a simmer.

5. Cover the pan and cook for 20 minutes, or until the rice is al dente and most of the liquid is absorbed.

6. Stir in the peas, place the mussels on top, and cover the skillet. Cook until the mussels open, about 3 minutes. Discard any mussels that don't open; serve hot.

# SPICY TEQUILA-LIME SHRIMP LETTUCE WRAPS

**10″ SKILLET, SHEET PAN** / Gluten-Free / Grain-Free / One Pan / Quick & Easy

**Serves 2 to 4 / Prep time: 5 minutes, plus 15 minutes to marinate /
Cook time: 5 minutes**

Lettuce cups or wraps are one of the easiest gluten-free, low-carb meals you could make. But they can also get boring, quick. These cups are full of bold flavors such as spicy jalapeño peppers, zesty lime, tequila, and spices. They're a perfect grain-free addition to your Taco Tuesday (yes, tequila is grain-free). Best of all, this recipe comes together in under 25 minutes. And 15 of those minutes are spent just waiting for the shrimp to marinate in the refrigerator.

| | |
|---|---|
| 2 tablespoons extra-virgin olive oil, divided | 1 pound medium raw shrimp, peeled and deveined |
| 3 tablespoons tequila | Salt |
| 3 tablespoons freshly squeezed lime juice | Freshly ground black pepper |
| 1 tablespoon honey | Butter, Bibb, or romaine lettuce |
| ½ teaspoon chili powder | Sliced avocado, for topping |
| ¼ teaspoon ground cumin | Whole-fat sour cream, for topping |
| 2 garlic cloves, thinly sliced | Chopped fresh cilantro, for topping |
| 1 jalapeño pepper, thinly sliced | Fresh lime, for topping |

1.  In a small bowl, whisk 1 tablespoon of olive oil with the tequila, lime juice, honey, chili powder, cumin, garlic, and jalapeño pepper. Stir in the shrimp, cover, and let marinate in the refrigerator for 15 minutes.

2.  Preheat the skillet over medium heat. Heat the remaining tablespoon of olive oil, and add the shrimp and marinade. Cook until the marinade is bubbling and the shrimp are pink, about 2 minutes per side. Season with salt and pepper.

3.  Fill the lettuce cups with the shrimp, top with sliced avocado, sour cream, cilantro, and lime juice, and serve.

**VARIATION TIP:** This recipe is still delicious without the tequila, if you prefer not to use it.

# CHICKEN WITH PEARS AND BUTTERNUT SQUASH

**12" SKILLET** / Gluten-Free / Grain-Free / One Pan / Weeknight

Serves 4 / Prep time: 10 minutes / Cook time: 30 minutes

Sweet fruit can really balance out recipes, especially when caramelized. Here, ripe pears caramelize in honey and butter and pair perfectly with golden seared chicken, butternut squash, wine, and herbs.

4 boneless, skinless chicken breasts (about 8 ounces each)

Salt

Freshly ground black pepper

2 tablespoons extra-virgin olive oil

2 tablespoons unsalted butter

1 leek, white and light green parts only, thinly sliced

2 garlic cloves, minced

1 small butternut squash, peeled, seeded, and cubed

2 pears, peeled, cored, and sliced

½ cup white wine

1 teaspoon Dijon mustard

1 tablespoon honey

½ cup chicken stock

2 teaspoons chopped fresh rosemary

1 tablespoon chopped fresh sage

1. Preheat the skillet over medium heat, and season both sides of the chicken breasts with salt and pepper.

2. Heat the olive oil in the skillet. Sear the chicken breasts until browned on both sides and cooked through (to an internal temperature of 165°F), about 6 minutes per side. Transfer to a plate and set aside.

3. In the skillet, melt the butter. Add the leek and sauté until golden and softened, 3 to 5 minutes. Add the garlic and cook for another minute.

4. Add the butternut squash and pears, season with salt and pepper, and cook until the squash begins to soften and the pears start to get golden at the edges, 6 to 8 minutes.

5. Deglaze the skillet with the wine, using a wooden spoon to scrape up any browned bits from the bottom of the pan. Let the wine bubble for 1 to 2 minutes, until slightly reduced.

6. Stir in the Dijon, honey, chicken stock, rosemary, and sage. Let the sauce bubble, and cook until the squash is tender, about 5 minutes. Return the chicken to the skillet for 2 to 3 minutes to warm through before serving.

# CHICKEN POT PIE WITH PUFF PASTRY BISCUITS

**12″ SKILLET** / One Pan / Weeknight

**Serves 6 / Prep time: 10 minutes / Cook time: 50 minutes**

A chicken pot pie can be an all-day affair, especially if you're making the stock and the pie crust. I've done that—and while, yes, it tastes amazing, sometimes you crave comfort food on a cold Monday night with only an hour to spare. On nights like those, this pot pie is your best friend. Chicken thighs cook quickly in a simple gravy of wine, stock, cream, and herbs. Skip the pie crust and cut out biscuits from frozen puff pastry for a fun, flaky spin.

2 tablespoons extra-virgin olive oil, divided

1½ pounds boneless, skinless chicken thighs

Salt

Freshly ground black pepper

2 tablespoons unsalted butter

1 leek, white and light green parts only, sliced

1 onion, diced

2 carrots, peeled and diced

1 parsnip, peeled and diced

2 celery stalks, diced

2 cups peeled and diced potato

2 garlic cloves, minced

2 tablespoons all-purpose flour

¼ cup white wine

¾ cup fresh or frozen peas

¾ cup fresh or frozen corn

1 teaspoon dried thyme

2 cups chicken broth

½ cup heavy (whipping) cream

1 package frozen puff pastry, thawed

1 large egg, beaten

1. Preheat the oven to 400°F, and place the skillet over medium heat.

2. Heat 1 tablespoon of olive oil in the skillet, and season both sides of the chicken thighs with salt and pepper. Add the thighs to the hot skillet and sear until browned and cooked through, about 5 minutes per side. Transfer to a plate and set aside.

3. Add the remaining tablespoon of olive oil and the butter to the hot skillet. Add the leek and onion and sauté until translucent, 5 to 7 minutes. Stir in the carrots, parsnip, celery, potato, and garlic. Cook until the vegetables are nearly softened, about 5 minutes, then sprinkle with the flour and cook for 2 to 3 minutes more.

4. Deglaze the pan with the wine, using a wooden spoon to scrape up any browned bits from the bottom. Stir in the peas, corn, thyme, chicken broth, and cream. Cook the mixture until bubbling and thickened. Season with salt and pepper. Dice the chicken thighs into medium chunks and stir them into the filling.

5. Roll the thawed puff pastry out slightly, and cut it into circles using a large biscuit cutter. Poke holes in each puff pastry biscuit, using a fork.

6. Cover the filling with the puff pastry circles. Brush with the egg and transfer to the oven. Bake until the puff pastry is golden brown, about 25 minutes. Serve warm.

**VARIATION TIP:** If you have a little bit more time on hand, try making the Sweet Potato Biscuits on page 52. Top this pot pie with the biscuits instead of the puff pastry, and bake until golden brown.

# AFRICAN CHICKEN STEW

**MEDIUM DUTCH OVEN** / Gluten-Free / One Pan

Serves 6 to 8 / Prep time: 10 minutes / Cook time: 50 minutes

This unique sweet and savory stew includes tender pieces of chicken, black-eyed peas, tomatoes, sweet potatoes, and peanut butter.

2 tablespoons extra-virgin olive oil or coconut oil

1½ pounds boneless, skinless chicken thighs

Salt

Freshly ground black pepper

1 yellow onion, diced

2 carrots, peeled and diced

4 garlic cloves, minced

1 tablespoon grated fresh ginger

1 sweet potato, peeled and cubed

1 (15-ounce) can black-eyed peas, drained and rinsed

1 (28-ounce) can crushed tomatoes

½ teaspoon ground cumin

½ teaspoon ground coriander

½ teaspoon smoked paprika

1 cup chicken broth

⅓ cup creamy peanut butter

Cooked brown rice, for serving

Chopped fresh cilantro, for serving

Chopped roasted peanuts, for serving

1.  Preheat the Dutch oven over medium heat with the oil. Once the oil is hot, season the chicken thighs on both sides with salt and pepper and add them to the pot. Cook until browned on both sides and cooked through, about 5 minutes per side. Transfer to a plate and set aside.

2.  Add the onion, carrots, and garlic to the pot and cook until softened, 5 to 7 minutes. Stir in the ginger and sweet potato.

3.  Add the black-eyed peas, tomatoes, cumin, coriander, and smoked paprika to the pot. Season with salt and pepper.

4.  In a small bowl, whisk together the chicken broth and peanut butter. Add this mixture to the pot, and bring the stew to a simmer. Once simmering, add the chicken thighs (cubed or left whole) back to the pot.

5.  Cover with a lid and cook until the vegetables and chicken are tender, 35 to 40 minutes.

6.  Serve over rice with chopped fresh cilantro and peanuts on top.

**SUBSTITUTION TIP:** You can use sunbutter or cashew butter in place of peanut butter.

# LEMON CHICKEN WITH FARRO AND ZA'ATAR

**12" SKILLET, SMALL DUTCH OVEN OR POT** / Weeknight

**Serves 4 / Prep time: 5 minutes / Cook time: 45 minutes**

This dish takes your everyday lemon chicken to new and unique heights. One-pot farro is used in place of rice for a wonderfully hearty texture. We also forgo your typical Italian seasonings for za'atar, a Middle Eastern spice blend made from sesame seeds, sumac, salt, and thyme.

2 tablespoons extra-virgin olive oil, divided

4 boneless, skinless chicken breasts (about 8 ounces each)

1 tablespoon za'atar

2 lemons, 1 cut into wedges and 1 zested and juiced, divided

1 shallot, diced

3 garlic cloves, minced

1½ cups dry pearled farro

3 cups chicken stock

Salt

Freshly ground black pepper

Whole-fat Greek yogurt or tzatziki, for serving

1. Preheat the oven to 375°F, and place the skillet over medium heat.

2. In the skillet, heat 1 tablespoon of olive oil. Evenly season each side of the chicken with the za'atar blend.

3. Add the chicken to the hot skillet and cook until browned, about 3 minutes per side.

4. Tuck the lemon wedges around the chicken breasts. Transfer the skillet to the oven and bake until the chicken is browned and cooked through, 20 to 30 minutes, depending on the size of the breasts.

5. Meanwhile, in a small Dutch oven or pot, heat the remaining tablespoon of olive oil. Add the shallot and garlic and cook until just softened, 3 to 5 minutes. Add the farro and toss to coat.

6. Add the chicken stock, and let it come to a simmer. Cover and simmer until the farro is tender but slightly chewy and the stock is absorbed, about 30 minutes.

7. Uncover the pot and stir in the lemon juice and zest. Season with salt and pepper.

8. Serve the chicken over the farro with Greek yogurt.

# EASY SPICY CHICKEN TORTILLA SOUP

**MEDIUM DUTCH OVEN** / Gluten-Free / One Pan / Weeknight

**Serves 8 / Prep time: 10 minutes / Cook time: 40 minutes**

When I was growing up, my family was obsessed with a popular Mexican cantina chain restaurant. They all loved the fajitas and how you could hear them sizzling before they even reached your table, but I was there for the chicken tortilla soup. This easy soup comes together in 50 minutes and is made using only one pot—no cooking the chicken separately or blending required.

1 tablespoon avocado oil or extra-virgin olive oil

1 yellow onion, diced

1 jalapeño pepper, diced

1 red bell pepper, diced

4 garlic cloves, minced

Salt

Freshly ground black pepper

½ cup dry white wine

2 teaspoons ground cumin

1 teaspoon chipotle powder

1 teaspoon smoked paprika

½ teaspoon dried oregano

½ teaspoon ground coriander

1 (15-ounce) can tomato sauce

2 (14.5-ounce) cans fire-roasted diced tomatoes, undrained

4 cups chicken broth

2 cups frozen corn

1 (15-ounce) can black beans, drained and rinsed

1½ pounds boneless, skinless, chicken breast

⅓ cup chopped fresh cilantro

1. Preheat a Dutch oven with the oil until hot. Add the onion, jalapeño pepper, bell pepper, and garlic, and sauté until the vegetables are softened but not browned, about 5 minutes. Season with salt and pepper.

2. Add the white wine and continue cooking until the wine reduces by half, 2 to 3 minutes.

3. Add the cumin, chipotle powder, smoked paprika, oregano, and coriander. Stir and cook for 1 minute, until fragrant.

4. Add the tomato sauce, diced tomatoes and their juices, chicken broth, corn, and black beans.

5. Bring to a simmer, then add the chicken breasts. Cover and simmer for 20 minutes, until the chicken breasts are cooked through.

6. Remove the chicken from the soup and carefully shred it using two forks. Simmer the soup for another 5 to 10 minutes, uncovered, and stir the chicken back in just to warm it through.

7. Taste the soup for salt and seasoning, and adjust to taste. Stir in the fresh cilantro right before serving.

**SERVING TIP:** Serve this soup topped with sliced avocado, crushed corn tortilla chips, a scoop of sour cream, and fresh lime wedges.

# TURKEY MATZO BALL SOUP

**MEDIUM DUTCH OVEN** / One Pan

**Serves 6 to 8 / Prep time: 15 minutes / Cook time: 55 minutes**

This is my winter spin on a classic Jewish deli menu item—made with turkey, parsnips, and fresh herbs such as sage, rosemary, and thyme. Matzo balls are easy to make and only require a few ingredients. While most use chicken fat (schmaltz), vegetable oil or butter also work. I like to use club soda to ensure fluffy, tender matzo balls.

### FOR THE MATZO BALLS

1 cup matzo meal

1 teaspoon salt

¼ teaspoon freshly ground black pepper

½ teaspoon baking powder

4 large eggs

4 tablespoons (½ stick) melted unsalted butter

4 tablespoons club soda

### FOR THE SOUP

2 tablespoons extra-virgin olive oil

1 onion, diced

3 carrots, peeled and diced

2 parsnips, peeled and diced

3 celery stalks, sliced

2 garlic cloves, minced

Salt

Freshly ground black pepper

10 cups chicken broth

2 turkey breast tenderloins (about 1½ pounds total)

2 teaspoons chopped fresh rosemary

1 tablespoon chopped fresh sage

1 teaspoon chopped fresh thyme

### TO MAKE THE MATZO BALLS

1. In a small bowl, whisk together the matzo meal, salt, pepper, and baking powder. In a medium bowl, whisk the eggs until beaten, then whisk in the melted butter and club soda. Add the dry ingredients to the wet mixture, and stir until evenly combined.

2. Refrigerate, uncovered, for at least 30 minutes while you start the soup.

### TO MAKE THE SOUP

1. Preheat the Dutch oven over medium heat. Heat the olive oil, and stir the onion, carrots, parsnips, and celery. Cook until the onions are translucent and the vegetables are beginning to soften, 8 to 10 minutes. Stir in the garlic and cook for another minute. Season with salt and pepper.

2. Pour in the chicken broth, and bring to a simmer.

3. Once simmering, add the turkey tenderloins to the pot, submerge them in the broth, and cover with a lid. Poach the turkey until it is cooked through and the internal temperature reaches 165°F, about 15 minutes. Using tongs, transfer the turkey to a plate; set aside.

4. Remove the matzo dough from the refrigerator and, using your hands, shape it into 8 golf ball–size balls. Drop them into the simmering pot of soup and replace the lid. Cook for 25 to 30 minutes, until the matzo balls are floating and cooked through.

5. Shred the turkey breasts and return them to the soup, along with the rosemary, sage, and thyme. Taste, adjust the seasonings, and serve.

**COOKING TIP:** This soup is a great use for leftover turkey; just add 4 cups of cooked shredded or cubed turkey to the soup during the last 5 minutes of cooking.

# CREAMY TUSCAN CHICKEN WITH ORZO

**12" SKILLET** / One Pan / Weeknight

**Serves 4 / Prep time: 10 minutes / Cook time: 35 minutes**

This meal is effortless enough for a weeknight dinner but impressive enough to serve guests. It comes together quickly using simple, flavorful ingredients like sun-dried tomatoes, herbs, cheese, and cream. I like to serve this dish over orzo pasta, which cooks quickly and in perfect timing as you prepare the chicken.

3 tablespoons extra-virgin olive oil, divided

4 boneless, skinless chicken breasts

Salt

Freshly ground black pepper

1 tablespoon unsalted butter

1 yellow onion, diced

8 ounces cremini mushrooms, sliced

3 garlic cloves, minced

2 Roma tomatoes, seeded and diced

⅓ cup sliced sun-dried tomatoes

½ teaspoon dried oregano

½ teaspoon dried thyme

1 cup heavy (whipping) cream

5 ounces baby spinach

½ cup grated Parmesan cheese, plus more for serving

¼ cup chopped fresh basil, plus more for serving

2½ cups cooked orzo pasta (1 cup dry)

1. Preheat the skillet over medium heat, and heat 2 tablespoon of olive oil. Season both sides of the chicken with salt and pepper, and add to the skillet. Cook until browned and cooked through, about 6 minutes per side, depending on thickness. Transfer to a plate to rest.

2. Add the remaining tablespoon of olive oil and the butter to the skillet. Add the onion and cook until golden and translucent, about 5 minutes. Add the mushrooms and cook until softened and golden, about 5 minutes. Stir in the garlic and cook for another minute, until fragrant. Add the diced tomatoes and sun-dried tomatoes. Season with the oregano and thyme.

3. Stir in the cream, and bring the mixture to a low simmer. Stir in the spinach and cook until wilted, about 3 minutes. Simmer until thickened, 2 to 3 minutes, and stir in the Parmesan cheese and basil. Taste and season with salt and pepper, if needed. Return the chicken to the pan to coat it in the sauce and heat it through.

4. Serve over cooked orzo with additional basil and Parmesan cheese on top.

# HEALTHY TURKEY BEAN CHILI

**MEDIUM DUTCH OVEN** / Gluten-Free / One Pan / Weeknight

**Serves 8 / Prep time: 10 minutes / Cook time: 50 minutes**

What's more comforting than a bowl of hearty chili on a cold night? This high-protein, fiber-rich recipe calls for lean turkey and a plethora of vegetables. I like to serve it over brown rice with sliced avocado and a scoop of Greek yogurt, making this a satisfying comfort food you can feel good about eating. My secret ingredient is unsweetened cocoa powder, which adds warmth and balances all the spices.

2 tablespoons extra-virgin olive oil

1 yellow onion, diced

2 celery stalks, diced

2 large carrots, peeled and diced

1 red bell pepper, diced

3 garlic cloves, minced

Salt

Freshly ground black pepper

1 pound ground turkey breast

2 tablespoons chili powder

2 teaspoons ground cumin

2 teaspoons dried oregano

¼ teaspoon ground cayenne pepper

1 tablespoon unsweetened
  cocoa powder

½ teaspoon paprika

Pinch crushed red pepper flakes

1 (28-ounce) can diced tomatoes

1 cup chicken broth

1 (15-ounce) can kidney beans, drained
  and rinsed

1 (15-ounce) can black beans, drained
  and rinsed

1½ cups fresh or frozen corn

1. Preheat the Dutch oven over medium heat, and heat the olive oil. Add the onion, celery, carrots, bell pepper, and garlic; sauté until the vegetables are softened but not browned, about 7 minutes. Season with salt and pepper.

2. Add the turkey and cook, breaking it up with a wooden spoon, until browned and no longer pink, about 10 minutes.

3. Stir in the chili powder, cumin, oregano, cayenne, cocoa powder, paprika, and red pepper flakes. Cook for 2 minutes, until fragrant.

4. Add the diced tomatoes, chicken broth, beans, and corn, and bring to a simmer. Reduce the heat, cover, and simmer for about 30 minutes to let the chili thicken and deepen its flavors.

5. Serve with desired toppings.

# TURKEY TAMALE PIE WITH CORNBREAD CRUMBLE

**12″ SKILLET** / One Pan

**Serves 6 to 8 / Prep time: 10 minutes / Cook time: 1 hour**

Tamale pie is a classic Southwestern casserole filled with meat, beans, corn, tomatoes, and plenty of spices. It's topped with a cornbread batter, and everything gets baked until golden. While I love a traditional tamale pie, my spin on it calls for a buttery, crisp, and savory streusel-like topping that adds plenty of texture.

## FOR THE TURKEY

2 tablespoons extra-virgin olive oil

1 yellow onion, diced

1 pound ground turkey

Salt

Freshly ground black pepper

1 red bell pepper, diced

2 garlic cloves, minced

1 tablespoon chili powder

1 teaspoon ground cumin

1 tablespoon tomato paste

¾ cup chicken stock

1 (15-ounce) can diced fire-roasted tomatoes

1 (15-ounce) can black beans, drained and rinsed

1 cup fresh or frozen corn

## FOR THE CRUMBLE

½ cup fine- or medium-grind cornmeal

½ cup all-purpose flour

1 tablespoon sugar

1 teaspoon salt

½ teaspoon baking powder

4 tablespoons (½ stick) cold unsalted butter, cubed

1 large egg

2 tablespoons extra-virgin olive oil

## FOR ASSEMBLING AND SERVING

1 cup shredded sharp Cheddar cheese

Sliced avocado, sliced pickled jalapeño peppers, and fresh cilantro, for serving

### TO MAKE THE TURKEY

1. Preheat the oven to 350°F. Preheat the skillet over medium heat.

2. In the skillet, heat the olive oil. Add the onion and cook until golden and translucent, about 6 minutes. Add the ground turkey and break it up with a wooden spoon. Season with salt and pepper and cook the turkey until browned, about 10 minutes.

3.  Add the bell pepper, garlic, chili powder, and cumin. Cook for 2 minutes, stir in the tomato paste, and cook for another minute. Deglaze the pan with the chicken stock, using a spoon to scrape up the browned bits from the bottom, and let the mixture come to a simmer.

4.  Once the chicken stock has reduced a bit, after a few minutes, stir in the tomatoes, beans, and corn. Let the mixture simmer for 10 minutes to thicken. Season with more salt and pepper.

**TO MAKE THE CRUMBLE**

While the filling simmers, in a medium bowl, mix together the cornmeal, flour, sugar, salt, and baking powder. Using a fork or pastry cutter, cut in the cold butter cubes until they are broken up into pea-size pieces. In a small bowl, whisk the egg with the olive oil until combined. Stir this mixture into the cornmeal until a dough forms.

**TO ASSEMBLE AND SERVE**

1.  Remove the turkey mixture from the heat, and fold in the shredded cheese.

2.  Break up the crumble dough into streusel and evenly top the entire surface of the turkey.

3.  Transfer the tamale pie to the oven and bake until the topping is golden and the mixture is bubbly, about 30 minutes.

4.  Serve topped with sliced avocado, sliced pickled jalapeño peppers, and fresh cilantro.

**VARIATION TIP:** Feel free to use beef here in place of turkey. You can boost the spice by adding 1 diced jalapeño pepper or using 2 cups of spicy salsa in place of the diced tomatoes.

*Cajun Andouille Sausage
and Shrimp Quinoa Skillet
page 146*

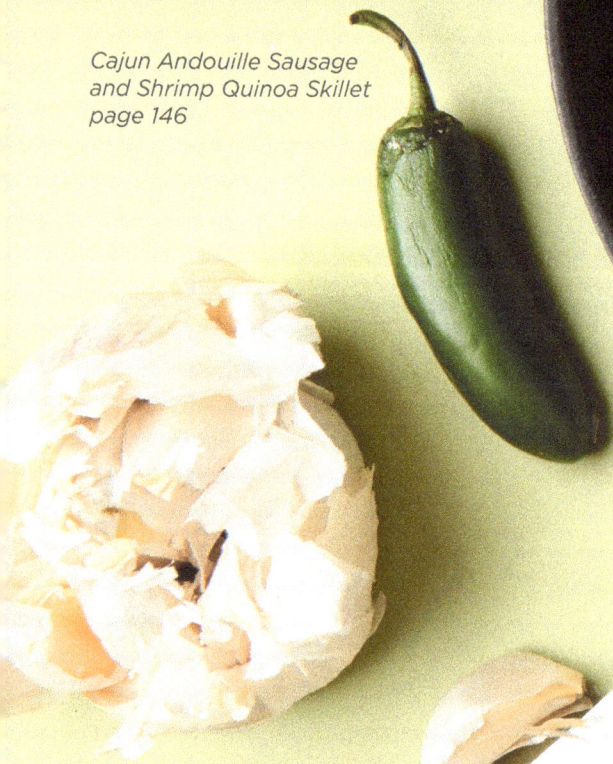

# chapter seven

## BEEF, PORK & LAMB

# MISO MEATBALLS WITH SLAW

**12" SKILLET** / Quick & Easy

**Serves 4 to 6 / Prep time: 15 minutes / Cook time: 15 minutes**

Miso, a fermented soybean paste, deserves more use in your kitchen beyond soup. This flavorful ingredient can be found at Whole Foods, Asian markets, and most grocery stores, too. Other than miso, this recipe calls for mostly refrigerator and pantry staples, which combine to form an intensely flavorful dish that's ready in 30 minutes.

## FOR THE SLAW

2 cups shredded cabbage

1 cup shredded carrot

¼ cup chopped fresh cilantro

½ lime, juiced

1 scallion, green parts only, sliced

1 jalapeño pepper, sliced

2 tablespoons extra-virgin olive oil

1 tablespoon rice vinegar

2 tablespoons sesame seeds

Salt

Freshly ground black pepper

## FOR THE MEATBALLS

2 garlic cloves, minced

1 tablespoon sesame oil

2 tablespoons white miso

2 tablespoons whole milk

1 large egg

¾ teaspoon salt

2 scallions, green parts only,
   finely chopped

1 tablespoon plus 1 teaspoon grated
   fresh ginger, divided

2 pinches crushed red pepper
   flakes, divided

¼ cup panko bread crumbs

1 pound ground beef

Vegetable oil, for frying

¼ cup soy sauce

2 tablespoons honey

1 tablespoon rice vinegar

1 teaspoon toasted sesame seeds

### TO MAKE THE SLAW

In a large bowl, toss together the cabbage, carrot, cilantro, lime juice, scallion, jalapeño pepper, olive oil, rice vinegar, and sesame seeds. Season with salt and pepper, and set aside for 15 minutes to let the flavors meld and the cabbage soften.

### TO MAKE THE MEATBALLS

1. Preheat the oven to 400°F, and place the skillet over medium heat.

2. In a medium bowl, mix together the garlic, sesame oil, miso, milk, egg, salt, scallions, 1 tablespoon of ginger, and the red pepper flakes. Add the panko and beef and mix until just incorporated, taking care not to overmix.

3. Preheat about ¼ inch of oil in the skillet. Using a 1-ounce scoop, form the mixture into 15 meatballs. Brown the meatballs in the hot oil, 1 to 2 minutes per side, working in two batches. Once all the meatballs are browned, pour out the oil and return the meatballs to the skillet. Transfer to the oven and bake until cooked through, 6 to 8 minutes.

4. Meanwhile, in a small bowl, whisk together the soy sauce, honey, rice vinegar, remaining 1 teaspoon of ginger, sesame seeds, and a pinch red pepper flakes. Pour the sauce over the meatballs as soon as they come out of the oven, and let the sauce bubble in the hot skillet before tossing to coat the meatballs. If needed, return the skillet to low heat to thicken the sauce.

5. Serve the slaw alongside the meatballs.

**VARIATION TIP:** The slaw, while delicious, is optional. You could also serve these meatballs over rice or with steamed broccoli.

# HORSERADISH-CRUSTED STEAKS

**12″ SKILLET** / 5-Ingredient / One Pan / Quick & Easy

Serves 2 / Prep time: 5 minutes / Cook time: 10 minutes

I know so many people who own a cast iron skillet for one reason and one reason only: cooking steak. While I think cast iron is wonderful for many things, this is especially true for cooking the perfect steak. Once I began making steak in cast iron, it was inconceivable to ever turn back. Nothing else will give you such a gorgeous sear and perfect crust with a juicy center. I worked at a popular chain steak house in high school for several years, and this recipe is inspired by their horseradish steak. I recommend the well-marbled but tender rib eye filet for this recipe.

Extra-virgin olive oil, for greasing

2 tablespoons prepared horseradish

3 tablespoons unsalted butter, melted

¼ cup panko bread crumbs

1 teaspoon salt

½ teaspoon freshly ground black pepper

2 garlic cloves, finely minced

2 (8-ounce) rib eye filet or filet mignon steaks

1. Preheat the oven to 500°F, and place a lightly oiled skillet over medium heat.

2. In a small bowl, combine the horseradish, melted butter, panko, salt, pepper, and garlic.

3. Season the steaks on both sides with salt and pepper. Add the steaks to the hot skillet and sear until a golden crust has formed, 1 to 2 minutes per side.

4. Top each steak evenly with half of the panko mixture, pressing down to adhere it to the steak.

5. Transfer the skillet to the oven and bake until the crust is golden brown and the steak is cooked to your liking, 6 to 8 minutes for medium, and serve.

**VARIATION TIP:** Not a fan of horseradish? Use blue cheese, Parmesan cheese, or a mixture of herbs in its place.

# REUBEN GRILLED CHEESE

**12" AND 10" SKILLETS OR GRILL PRESS** / 5-Ingredient / One Pan / Quick & Easy

**Serves 2 / Prep time: 5 minutes / Cook time: 10 minutes**

One of my favorite uses for cast iron skillets—aside from cooking in them, of course—is using them as a sandwich press. A 10-inch skillet is the perfect press when cooking sandwiches in a 12-inch skillet. Unlike an individual handheld cast iron grill press, a 10-inch skillet can weight down two sandwiches at once. This reuben comes together in about 15 minutes and requires only a handful of ingredients, making it one of the fastest crowd-pleasing meals around.

½ **pound thinly sliced corned beef**

4 **tablespoons Thousand Island dressing**
 **(see tip)**

4 **rye bread slices**

½ **cup sauerkraut**

**Salt**

**Freshly ground black pepper**

4 **Swiss cheese slices**

2 **tablespoons unsalted butter**

1. Preheat the skillet over medium heat.

2. Add the corned beef to the hot skillet and, working in two batches, quickly brown each slice on both sides, 1 to 2 minutes per side. Set aside.

3. Spread 1 tablespoon of Thousand Island dressing evenly over each slice of bread.

4. Top each bottom slice of bread with hot corned beef (¼ pound per sandwich), followed by ¼ cup of sauerkraut. Season the sauerkraut with salt and pepper.

5. Top the sauerkraut with 2 slices of Swiss cheese and then cover with the top slice of bread.

6. Melt the butter in the skillet. Once hot, add the sandwiches. Press the sandwiches down with another skillet or a cast iron grill press. Cook until the sandwiches are golden on each side and the cheese is melted, about 3 minutes per side; serve immediately.

**INGREDIENT TIP:** To make your own Thousand Island dressing, combine ½ cup mayonnaise with 2 tablespoons ketchup, 2 tablespoons relish, 1 teaspoon apple cider vinegar, 1 tablespoon minced onion, and 1 teaspoon minced garlic. Season with salt.

# STEAK WITH STROGANOFF MUSHROOM SAUCE

**12″ SKILLET** / Gluten-Free / One Pan / Weeknight

**Serves 3 or 4 / Prep time: 10 minutes / Cook time: 25 minutes**

My mom makes the best stroganoff. It's an all-day event, or more if you count her trip to the butcher for the perfect cuts. Her stroganoff is so tender and comforting, and quite possibly my "desert island" pick of winter food. I like to make this much quicker version when I'm missing my mom. Perfectly seared steak is sliced and served atop golden brown mushrooms swimming in a buttery, flavorful sauce.

2 tablespoons extra-virgin olive oil, divided

1½ pounds sirloin steak

Salt

Freshly ground black pepper

2 tablespoons unsalted butter

1 shallot, minced

1 pound cremini mushrooms, thinly sliced

2 garlic cloves, minced

⅓ cup white wine

¼ cup vegetable stock

1 tablespoon cornstarch

2 teaspoons Worcestershire sauce (gluten-free if needed)

½ cup whole-fat sour cream or Greek yogurt

Chopped fresh dill or parsley, for serving

1.  Preheat the skillet over medium heat, and heat 1 tablespoon of olive oil.

2.  Season both sides of the steak with salt and pepper, and add to the hot skillet. Cook until both sides are browned and cooked just below your desired doneness, 3 to 4 minutes per side for medium rare.

3.  Transfer the steak to a plate; set it aside to rest.

4. Add the additional tablespoon of olive oil and the butter to the hot skillet. Once the butter is melted and bubbling, stir in the shallot and cook until just softened, about 5 minutes.

5. Stir in the mushrooms and cook until they begin to brown and soften, 5 to 7 minutes. Season with salt and pepper. Stir in the garlic and cook for about 1 minute, until fragrant. Deglaze the pan with the white wine, using a wooden spoon to scrape up the browned bits from the bottom. Let the wine simmer and reduce for 2 to 3 minutes.

6. In a small bowl, whisk together the vegetable stock and cornstarch until the cornstarch is dissolved. Add the stock mixture to the skillet, along with the Worcestershire sauce; simmer for another few minutes, until the sauce is thickened.

7. Taste the sauce and adjust for seasoning. Turn off the heat and stir in the sour cream until combined and warmed through.

8. Slice the steak and divide it among plates. Top with the mushroom sauce, garnish with fresh dill, and serve.

**COOKING TIP:** Never add a cold steak straight from the refrigerator to your cast iron skillet. Take the steak out of the refrigerator and let it sit at room temperature for 30 minutes before searing. Pat the steak dry with paper towels before seasoning.

# SWEET POTATO-BEEF CHILI

**MEDIUM DUTCH OVEN** / Gluten-Free / Grain-Free / One Pan / Weeknight

Serves 6 / Prep time: 10 minutes / Cook time: 50 minutes

I created this recipe when I was in the middle of doing a Whole30 and following a strict gluten-, grain-, dairy-, and sugar-free diet. I posted a photo of this chili on Instagram, and a popular cooking magazine reposted it. I soon had hundreds of direct messages asking me for the recipe. Healthy, hearty, and delicious, this is a recipe I continue to make, whether I'm on Whole30 or not.

1 tablespoon extra-virgin olive oil

1 red onion, diced

1½ pounds 85% lean grass-fed ground beef

Salt

Freshly ground black pepper

2 carrots, peeled and diced

1 red bell pepper, diced

1 leek, white and light green parts only, diced

2 sweet potatoes, peeled and large diced

4 garlic cloves, minced

1 tablespoon tomato paste

1 tablespoon chili powder

1 teaspoon smoked paprika

2 teaspoons ground cumin

½ teaspoon dried oregano

½ teaspoon dried thyme

2 dried bay leaves

¼ teaspoon crushed red pepper flakes

2 (14.5-ounce) cans diced fire-roasted tomatoes

2 cups beef bone broth

Sliced avocado, sliced pepperoncinis, and chopped fresh cilantro, for serving

1. Preheat the Dutch oven over medium heat, and heat the olive oil. When the oil is hot, add the red onion and cook until slightly softened, about 3 minutes. Stir in the ground beef, and season with salt and pepper. Break up the beef with a wooden spoon and cook until browned, about 8 minutes.

2. Add the carrots, bell pepper, leek, sweet potatoes, and garlic. Cook until the vegetables are starting to soften, about 5 minutes.

3. Stir in the tomato paste, chili powder, paprika, cumin, oregano, thyme, bay leaves, and red pepper flakes. Cook for 1 minute more.

4. Add the diced tomatoes and bone broth. Bring to a simmer.

5. Cover and let simmer for 30 minutes. You can uncover it after about 20 minutes to let some of the liquid reduce for a thicker chili.

6. Discard the bay leaves before serving, and taste and adjust for seasoning. Serve topped with avocado, pepperoncinis, and cilantro.

**VARIATION TIP:** For a leaner chili, replace the beef with ground turkey or chicken.

# LOMO SALTADO (PERUVIAN STEAK AND POTATO STIR-FRY)

**12″ SKILLET**/ Gluten-Free / Grain-Free / Weeknight

**Serves 4 / Prep time: 10 minutes / Cook time: 35 minutes**

My cousin Angela is half Peruvian, and she introduced me to lomo saltado, a delicious steak stir-fry made with peppers, vinegar, tomatoes, soy sauce, and everyone's favorite: French fries. Typically, the French fries are tossed in with the stir-fry, and frozen fries work just fine here. Either fry them in a skillet or cook them in the oven before tossing into the stir-fry.

2 tablespoons extra-virgin olive oil, divided

1 pound sirloin steak

Salt

Freshly ground black pepper

1 red onion, sliced

1 yellow bell pepper, sliced

2 garlic cloves, minced

1 jalapeño pepper, thinly sliced

3 plum tomatoes, halved, seeded, and sliced

½ teaspoon ground cumin

2 tablespoons tamari soy sauce

2 tablespoons apple cider vinegar

1 pound prepared French fries (see headnote)

Chopped fresh cilantro, for serving

1. Preheat the skillet over medium heat. Heat 1 tablespoon of olive oil, and season both sides of the steak with salt and pepper. Add the steak to the skillet and sear for 3 to 4 minutes per side. Set aside to rest.

2. Add the remaining tablespoon of oil to the skillet, along with the onion. Cook the onion until golden and caramelized, about 10 minutes.

3. Add the bell pepper, garlic, and jalapeño pepper. Season with salt and pepper. Cook until the vegetables are softened and golden, about 7 minutes, and stir in the tomatoes. Sprinkle on the cumin.

4. Add the soy sauce and vinegar to the skillet and let the mixture sizzle. Thinly slice the steak and return it to the pan. Cook to your desired doneness.

5. Remove from the heat and toss in the hot French fries. Serve topped with fresh cilantro.

**INGREDIENT TIP:** Tamari is a wheat-free soy sauce that keeps this dish gluten-free, but you can use any soy sauce you'd like. Use coconut aminos to make this dish paleo.

# BRATWURST WITH CABBAGE, POTATOES, AND BEER-MUSTARD SAUCE

**12" SKILLET**/ One Pan / Weeknight

**Serves 4 / Prep time: 10 minutes / Cook time: 40 minutes**

I love a great German beer hall. The food is simple, the beer is cold, and the ambiance is lively. One of my favorite German dishes is bratwurst with mustard. There's always a different version of this on beer hall menus. Some serve it on a sandwich with a beer mustard and sauerkraut, and some serve it with roasted cabbage and potatoes or fries. This recipe is the best of both worlds, and is best enjoyed with a cold pint.

2 tablespoons extra-virgin olive oil

4 bratwurst sausages

2 tablespoons unsalted butter

1 onion, thinly sliced

1 pound Yukon Gold potatoes, diced

1 small head green cabbage, quartered, cored, and thinly sliced

Salt

Freshly ground black pepper

½ teaspoon caraway seeds

1 cup dark beer

½ cup beef broth

2 tablespoons whole-grain Dijon mustard

¼ cup chopped fresh parsley

1. Preheat the skillet over medium heat, and heat the olive oil. Add the bratwurst and cook for 1 to 2 minutes per side, until browned, 6 to 8 minutes total. Transfer to a plate and cover with foil to keep warm.

2. Add the butter to the pan, followed by the onion. Sauté until the onion is soft and golden brown, 5 to 7 minutes. Stir in the potatoes and cabbage and cook until golden at the edges, 5 to 10 minutes. Season with salt and pepper, and add the caraway seeds.

3. When the potatoes and cabbage are almost tender, deglaze the pan with the beer, using a wooden spoon to scrape up the browned bits from the bottom, and cook until the beer is reduced by half, 3 to 5 minutes. Add the beef broth and mustard; bring to a simmer.

4. Return the bratwurst to the pan and cook, covered, for 5 minutes. Uncover and let cook until the sauce is thickened and the bratwurst is cooked through to an internal temperature of 160°F, 3 to 5 more minutes.

5. Garnish with the chopped parsley and serve.

# CARBONARA BAKED SPAGHETTI

**10″ SKILLET, LARGE POT** / Weeknight

Serves 6 to 8 / Prep time: 10 minutes / Cook time: 50 minutes

My dad and I went through a major carbonara phase after watching his favorite chef make it on TV. Nowadays I like to switch it up by making this spaghetti pie. Pasta, pancetta, aromatics like onion and garlic, spinach, wine, and Parmesan cheese all get coated in a creamy custard and baked in a cast iron skillet until set and crispy at the edges. This is a whimsical carbonara recipe that you can cut and serve like a pie, and guests always love it.

Salt

8 ounces dry spaghetti

2 tablespoons extra-virgin olive oil, divided

2 tablespoons unsalted butter, divided

½ onion, diced

5 ounces cubed pancetta

2 garlic cloves, minced

Freshly ground black pepper

¼ cup dry white wine

5 ounces baby spinach

2 large egg yolks

1 large egg

½ cup whole milk

⅓ cup heavy (whipping) cream

¼ teaspoon dried oregano

1 teaspoon chopped fresh thyme

1 cup grated Parmesan cheese, divided

Chopped fresh parsley, for serving

1.  Preheat the oven to 350°F. Place the skillet over medium heat.

2.  Bring a large pot of salted water to a boil, and cook the spaghetti according to package directions until al dente. Drain and transfer to a large bowl. Toss the spaghetti with 1 tablespoon of olive oil to keep it from sticking together.

3.  Meanwhile, heat 1 tablespoon of butter and the remaining tablespoon of olive oil in the skillet.

4.  Stir in the onion and cook until golden and translucent, 5 to 7 minutes. Push the onion to one side of the skillet and add the pancetta to the empty side of the skillet in one even layer. Brown the pancetta, stirring occasionally, until golden and crisp, about 5 minutes. Stir in the garlic and cook for an additional minute. Season with salt and pepper.

5. Deglaze the pan with the white wine, using a wooden spoon to scrape up the browned bits from the bottom, and let it bubble until nearly reduced, about 2 minutes. Stir in the spinach and cook until the greens are wilted, about 3 minutes.

6. Add the vegetable mixture to the spaghetti, and toss well to combine.

7. In a medium bowl, whisk together the egg yolks, egg, milk, cream, oregano, and thyme. Stir in 3/4 cup of Parmesan cheese.

8. Pour the custard mixture over the spaghetti, and toss to coat everything evenly in the bowl.

9. Melt the remaining 1 tablespoon of butter in the skillet, and swirl to grease the entire pan. Pour in the spaghetti, and press down with a spatula. Sprinkle the remaining ¼ cup of Parmesan cheese on top.

10. Transfer to the oven and bake until the custard is set and the edges and cheese on top are golden brown, 25 to 30 minutes.

11. Let cool slightly, and cut into 8 wedges. Top with parsley and serve.

**VARIATION TIP:** You can use bacon in place of pancetta and kale or broccoli rabe instead of spinach.

# BUTTERNUT SQUASH AND SAUSAGE MINESTRONE SOUP

**MEDIUM DUTCH OVEN, LARGE POT** / Weeknight

**Serves 8 / Prep time: 10 minutes / Cook time: 50 minutes**

The smell of minestrone soup reminds me of my grandma's house, where we would pour ladlefuls of piping hot minestrone into bowls and top it with far more Parmesan cheese than necessary. Minestrone is classic, comforting, and takes little effort. This fall-inspired version includes Italian sausage, butternut squash, and Swiss chard.

2 tablespoons extra-virgin olive oil, divided

Salt

1¼ cups dry ditalini pasta

1 pound mild Italian sausage, casings removed

Freshly ground black pepper

1 yellow onion, diced

2 celery stalks, diced

2 carrots, peeled and diced

4 garlic cloves, minced

1 tablespoon tomato paste

1 teaspoon dried thyme

¾ teaspoon dried oregano

1 tablespoon chopped fresh rosemary, plus more for serving

6 cups chicken broth

1 (28-ounce) can crushed tomatoes

2 dried bay leaves

2 (15-ounce) cans cannellini beans, drained and rinsed

1 butternut squash, peeled, seeded, and cut into ½-inch cubes

1 bunch Swiss chard, stemmed, leaves cut into thin ribbons

Shaved Parmesan cheese, for serving

1. Preheat a Dutch oven over medium heat, and heat 1 tablespoon olive oil. In a large pot, boil the pasta in salted water according to package directions until just barely al dente. Drain and set aside.

2. Add the ground sausage to the Dutch oven. Break it up with a wooden spoon, and season with salt and pepper. Cook until browned, about 10 minutes. Using a slotted spoon, transfer the sausage to a bowl and set aside.

3. Add the remaining tablespoon of olive oil to the pot, then add the onion, celery, and carrots. Cook until softened but not browned, about 3 minutes. Stir in the garlic and tomato paste and season with salt and pepper and the thyme, oregano, and rosemary.

4. Stir in the chicken broth, crushed tomatoes, bay leaves, beans, and butternut squash. Return the sausage to the pot, and bring the soup to a simmer.

5. Cover the soup and simmer until the butternut squash is cooked through, 15 to 20 minutes.

6. Uncover the pot and stir in the Swiss chard; cook until wilted and tender, about 5 minutes. Stir in the pasta, taste, and adjust the seasoning as needed.

7. Serve topped with shaved Parmesan cheese and additional rosemary.

**COOKING TIP:** I like to cook the pasta separately here to ensure that it's perfectly al dente. To keep this recipe one-pot, you can stir the dry pasta into the simmering soup for the last 10 minutes.

# PORK CHOPS WITH APPLE BUTTER AND FINGERLING POTATOES

**12" SKILLET** / Gluten-Free / Grain-Free / One Pan / Weeknight

**Serves 2 / Prep time: 10 minutes / Cook time: 35 minutes**

I wonder who first thought of pairing pork and apples. While this combination is classic, it is not boring. I love making this version in the fall. Sweet onion, fingerling potatoes, and apple in four forms (raw, butter, cider, and vinegar) make this a sweet, savory, and balanced weeknight dinner.

1 tablespoon extra-virgin olive oil

2 (½-pound) bone-in pork chops

Salt

Freshly ground black pepper

2 tablespoons unsalted butter

½ sweet onion, thinly sliced

½ pound fingerling potatoes, sliced

1 apple, peeled and thinly sliced

¼ cup apple butter

¼ cup apple cider

1 tablespoon apple cider vinegar

2 teaspoons chopped fresh rosemary

1. Place the skillet over medium heat, and preheat the oven to 400°F.

2. Heat the olive oil in the skillet. Season the pork chops with salt and pepper, and sear until browned, 3 minutes per side. Transfer to a plate and set aside to rest.

3. Melt the butter in the skillet. Add the onion and sauté until softened and golden, 5 to 7 minutes. Add the potatoes and apple and cook until browned and tender, about 8 minutes.

4. Stir in the apple butter, apple cider, and apple cider vinegar. Season with salt and pepper, and bring to a simmer. Stir in the rosemary.

5. Return the pork chops to the pan and transfer to the oven. Cook until the pork is cooked through and an internal thermometer reads 145°F, 10 to 15 minutes; serve hot.

**INGREDIENT TIP:** Apple butter is a thicker applesauce that is slowly cooked for a longer period of time until caramelized and deep, golden brown. You can find it at common grocery stores or natural grocers like Whole Foods.

# SPANISH PIZZA WITH MANCHEGO, JAMÓN, AND QUINCE

**12" SKILLET OR CAST IRON PIZZA PAN** / One Pan

**Serves 4 to 6 / Prep time: 10 minutes, plus 15 minutes to preheat /
Cook time: 10 minutes**

The most popular post on my blog is about creating your own at-home tapas party. This pizza combines all of my favorite tapas bites—manchego cheese, salty cured ham, quince paste, and olives. Imagine the perfect Spanish cheese board, but instead of crackers or bread, pizza crust is your foundation.

Flour, for dusting

12 ounces pizza dough

1 tablespoon extra-virgin olive oil

¼ cup quince paste

2 cups freshly shredded
  manchego cheese

3 ounces thinly sliced jamón (iberico
  or serrano)

⅓ cup sliced pimiento olives

1 teaspoon chopped fresh thyme

1 tablespoon chopped fresh rosemary

Honey, for drizzling

¼ teaspoon crushed red pepper flakes

1. Preheat the oven to 450°F, and place the pizza pan or skillet in it for 15 minutes.

2. Flour the preheated pan, and roll the pizza dough into a 12-inch circle. Place the pizza crust on the floured pan, and brush with the olive oil.

3. In a small microwavable bowl, warm the quince paste gently in the microwave; spread it evenly over the crust. Alternatively, you could cut the paste into thin strips or cubes and distribute it evenly on the crust.

4. Sprinkle the cheese evenly on top of the quince. Cut or tear the ham into short ribbons, and place it on top of the cheese. Scatter on the olives, thyme, and rosemary.

5. Transfer to the oven and bake until the crust is golden and the cheese is melted, about 12 minutes.

6. Drizzle honey over the hot pizza and top with the red pepper flakes before serving.

**INGREDIENT TIP:** You can find quince paste, also called membrillo, at Trader Joe's, Whole Foods, and international markets like Cost Plus World Market. It can also often be found at common grocers at their cheese counter. If you can't find it, try apple jelly instead.

# CAJUN ANDOUILLE SAUSAGE AND SHRIMP QUINOA SKILLET

**12" SKILLET** / Gluten-Free / One Pan / Weeknight

Serves 4 to 6 / Prep time: 10 minutes / Cook time: 35 minutes

I'm not sure what I love most about this skillet: the spicy Cajun flavors or how quickly it comes together. Quinoa is a unique addition, and best of all, there's no need to cook it separately. This skillet is quite spicy, but fresh cilantro and lemon juice balance the heat nicely.

2 tablespoons extra-virgin olive oil, divided

1 pound fully cooked andouille sausage, sliced

1 pound raw shrimp, peeled and deveined

Salt

Freshly ground black pepper

½ yellow onion, diced

1 jalapeño pepper, diced

1 red bell pepper, diced

2 garlic cloves, minced

1 (14.5-ounce) can diced fire-roasted tomatoes

1½ teaspoons Cajun seasoning

2 cups chicken stock

1 cup uncooked quinoa, rinsed

2 tablespoons freshly squeezed lemon juice

¼ cup chopped fresh cilantro

1. Preheat the skillet over medium heat. Heat 1 tablespoon of olive oil in the pan, and add the sliced sausage.

2. Brown the sausage evenly on both sides, about 5 minutes total. Transfer to a plate and set aside.

3. Add the shrimp to the hot skillet, and season with salt and pepper. Cook the shrimp until just pink, about 3 minutes. Transfer to the plate with the sausage and set aside.

4. Add the remaining tablespoon of olive oil to the skillet. Stir in the onion, jalapeño pepper, and bell pepper. Cook until the vegetables are lightly browned and just softened, 5 to 7 minutes. Season with salt and pepper.

5. Stir in the garlic and tomatoes with their juices, and bring to a simmer. Add the Cajun seasoning and simmer for 3 to 5 minutes.

6. Stir in the chicken stock and quinoa. Bring the mixture to a simmer and cover. Cook until the quinoa is tender and the liquid is absorbed, about 15 minutes.

7. Stir in the lemon juice and cilantro, and season with additional salt and pepper, if needed. Return the sausage and shrimp to the pan and heat through before serving.

**COOKING TIP:** This recipe works best in an enameled skillet with a lid, but it will still work in a regular skillet, uncovered. Just make sure that the quinoa is submerged in the liquid during cooking, and stir it often.

# JERSEY SHORE SAUSAGE SANDWICHES

**12" SKILLET, GRIDDLE OR SHEET PAN** / Weeknight

**Serves 4 / Prep time: 10 minutes / Cook time: 30 minutes**

I grew up in New Jersey, and (like everyone else in the state) we spent our summers "down the shore." I have fond memories of the Jersey shore, especially the food. After a long day at the beach, there was nothing better than a piping hot sausage sandwich on the boardwalk. This sandwich is made the same way, with both sweet and hot Italian sausage, peppers, onions, marinara, and melty cheese.

3 tablespoons extra-virgin olive oil, divided

1 pound sweet Italian sausage (4 links)

½ pound hot Italian sausage (2 links)

2 yellow onions, sliced

1 red bell pepper, sliced

1 orange bell pepper, sliced

3 garlic cloves, minced

¼ cup sliced pepperoncini peppers

½ teaspoon dried oregano

Salt

Freshly ground black pepper

2 tablespoons tomato paste

2 tablespoons red wine vinegar

1½ cups marinara sauce

4 Italian hoagie rolls

4 tablespoons (½ stick) unsalted butter, melted

1½ cups shredded mozzarella cheese or 8 provolone cheese slices (optional)

1. Place the skillet over medium heat, and preheat the oven to 350°F.

2. Heat 2 tablespoons of olive oil in the skillet. Pierce the sausage links with a fork, and add them to the skillet. Cook until browned on all sides and cooked through, about 10 minutes. Transfer to a plate and let rest.

3. Add the remaining tablespoon of oil to the skillet, along with the onions. Cook for 6 minutes to start caramelizing, then add the bell peppers and cook until golden, about 6 more minutes. Stir in the garlic, pepperoncini peppers, and oregano. Season with salt and pepper.

4. Stir in the tomato paste and cook for 2 minutes. Deglaze the pan with the vinegar, using a wooden spoon to scrape up the browned bits from the bottom. Stir in the tomato sauce.

5. Slice the sausages on the bias, and return them to the pan. Let the mixture simmer for 5 minutes. Taste and season with salt and pepper, if needed.

6. Brush the melted butter over the hoagies and toast them lightly, either in a griddle pan over medium heat or a sheet pan in a 350°F oven. Add the cheese to the hoagies (if using), fill the rolls with the sausage and sauce, and serve.

**VARIATION TIP:** To make this recipe dairy-free, skip the cheese (this sandwich has a lot of flavor without it) and brush the bread with olive oil instead of butter before toasting.

# LAMB CHOPS WITH MINT CHUTNEY

**12" SKILLET** / Gluten-Free / Grain-Free / One Pan / Quick & Easy

Serves 4 / Prep time: 10 minutes / Cook time: 5 minutes

From a weeknight dinner to an elegant dinner party, this quick, versatile recipe features a bright mint and cilantro chutney in place of your typical lamb-paired mint jelly. Jalapeño pepper adds heat to this chutney, but it's balanced out by fresh ginger, creamy yogurt, zesty lemon, and a touch of honey.

## FOR THE LAMB CHOPS

2 tablespoons extra-virgin olive oil

8 lamb loin chops (about
  2 pounds total)

Salt

Freshly ground black pepper

## FOR THE MINT CHUTNEY

½ cup chopped fresh cilantro

1 cup chopped fresh mint

1 jalapeño pepper, seeded and diced

2 garlic cloves, minced

1 teaspoon honey

2 teaspoons grated fresh ginger

1 tablespoon freshly squeezed
  lemon juice

Salt

Freshly ground black pepper

½ cup plain whole-fat Greek yogurt

### TO MAKE THE LAMB CHOPS

1. Preheat the skillet over medium heat. Heat the olive oil until shimmering. Season both sides of the lamb chops with salt and pepper.

2. Add the lamb chops to the skillet and sear until browned on both sides and a meat thermometer reads 135°F for medium, about 3 minutes per side.

3. Transfer to a plate, cover loosely with foil, and let the lamb rest for 5 minutes while you prepare the chutney.

### TO MAKE THE MINT CHUTNEY AND SERVE

1. In a food processor, combine the cilantro, mint, jalapeño pepper, garlic, honey, fresh ginger, and lemon juice. Blend until a thick paste forms. The chutney should be chunky, but you should not see large pieces of garlic or jalapeño pepper. Season with salt and pepper, and stir in the yogurt.

2. Serve the chutney with the lamb chops.

**SERVING TIP:** Serve this dish with homemade naan bread (page 44) or rice.

# LAMB SHEPHERD'S PIE WITH CAULIFLOWER-POTATO MASH

**12" SKILLET, LARGE POT**

**Serves 6 to 8 / Prep time: 15 minutes / Cook time: 50 minutes**

If you are intimidated by cooking lamb, ground lamb is a good place to start. One of the most common and classic uses for ground lamb is the shepherd's pie. This pie makes for a simple, healthy weeknight dinner. If you're not a fan of lamb, meats like beef or turkey will work, too.

1½ pounds russet potatoes, peeled and cut into chunks

¾ pound cauliflower, cut into florets

Salt

2 tablespoons extra-virgin olive oil

1 onion, diced

1 celery stalk, diced

2 carrots, peeled and diced

1 parsnip, peeled and diced

2 garlic cloves, minced

1 pound ground lamb

Freshly ground black pepper

1 tablespoon tomato paste

1 tablespoon Worcestershire sauce

½ cup beef bone broth

¾ cup fresh or frozen peas

2 teaspoons chopped fresh rosemary

½ cup whole milk

6 tablespoons (¾ stick) unsalted butter

1. Preheat the oven to 425°F, and place the skillet over medium heat.

2. Place the potatoes and cauliflower in a large pot, and cover with cold water. Salt the water and bring it to a boil. Cook until the potatoes and cauliflower are fork-tender, about 20 minutes.

3. Meanwhile, prepare the filling. Heat the olive oil in the skillet. Add the onion and cook until translucent and golden, 5 to 7 minutes. Stir in the celery, carrots, parsnip, and garlic, and continue cooking until the vegetables are nearly softened, about 5 minutes.

4. Add in the lamb, season with salt and pepper, and cook, breaking up the meat with a wooden spoon, for 3 minutes or until browned.

5. Stir in the tomato paste and Worcestershire, and cook for 1 minute. Deglaze the pan with the bone broth, using a spoon to scrape up the browned bits from the bottom. Bring the broth to a simmer and cook for 5 to 10 minutes, until slightly thickened. Stir in the peas and rosemary.

6. Taste for seasoning, and add more salt and pepper, if needed.

7. Drain the potato and cauliflower mixture. In a microwave-safe mug in the microwave or in a small saucepan on the stove over medium heat, warm the milk and butter. Mash the potatoes and cauliflower slightly with a potato masher or fork, add the warm butter-milk mixture, and generously season with salt and pepper. Continue mashing until smooth.

8. Top the lamb evenly with the potato and cauliflower mixture. Transfer to the oven and bake until the potatoes are golden, about 25 minutes; serve hot.

**INGREDIENT TIP:** Although less rich and thick than bone broth, beef broth or beef stock can be used here.

*Grilled Peaches with Hazelnuts and
Whipped Honey Mascarpone
page 160*

# chapter eight

# DESSERTS & SWEET TREATS

# GREEK YOGURT APPLE TARTE TATIN

**10" SKILLET** / One Pan / Vegetarian

**Serves 6 to 8 / Prep time: 20 minutes / Cook time: 1 hour, plus 15 minutes to cool**

Think of a tarte tatin as an upside-down apple pie—only easier. This dessert is meant to look rustic, and the flaky Greek yogurt pastry crust pairs perfectly with the caramelized apples. This tart is delicious served with frozen yogurt.

**FOR THE PASTRY CRUST**

1½ cups all-purpose flour, plus more
   for dusting

¼ teaspoon salt

1 tablespoon sugar

12 tablespoons (1½ sticks) cold
   unsalted butter

¼ cup cold plain whole-fat Greek yogurt

2 tablespoons ice-cold water

**FOR THE TARTE TATIN**

5 apples (Granny Smith or Pink Lady
   work well)

½ lemon, juiced

4 tablespoons (½ stick) unsalted butter

¾ cup sugar

Pinch salt

All-purpose flour, for dusting

Frozen yogurt, for serving

## TO MAKE THE PASTRY CRUST

1.  In a large bowl, combine the flour, salt, and sugar. Cut the cold butter into small, equal-size cubes. Using a pastry cutter or large fork, cut the butter into the flour until it is broken up into pea-size pieces.

2.  In a small bowl, whisk the cold water into the yogurt. Stir the yogurt into the butter-flour mixture until incorporated. The mixture will still be very crumbly.

3.  Knead the dough until it comes together. Turn out on a lightly floured surface and continue kneading until the dough forms a smooth ball.

4.  Chill until ready to roll out.

### TO MAKE THE TARTE TATIN

1.  Preheat the oven to 375°F, and place the skillet over medium heat.

2.  Peel, core, and quarter the apples. In a large bowl, toss them immediately with the lemon juice.

3.  In the skillet, combine the butter, sugar, and salt and cook until the butter is melted, the sugar is dissolved, and the mixture is a very light caramel color, 6 to 8 minutes.

4.  Arrange the apples in the skillet on top of the butter, cut-side down. Cook the apples in the caramel until they are beginning to soften and the sugar is caramelized and golden brown, 12 to 15 minutes.

5.  Turn the apples over so they are cut-side up (the rounded sides should be on the bottom, as the skillet will be flipped over once done) and both sides are coated in caramel. The apples will shrink significantly as they cook, so ensure that they are very closely packed and overlapping.

6.  On a lightly floured surface, roll out the pastry dough into a roughly 10-inch circle. Carefully lay the rolled dough on top of the skillet, tucking the edges inside the pan. Using a fork, poke holes over the crust. Transfer to the oven and bake until the crust is golden brown and crisp and the caramel is bubbling, about 40 minutes.

7.  Let the tart cool for 10 to 15 minutes, place a plate on top of the skillet, and carefully flip it over. Serve with frozen yogurt.

**COOKING TIP:** I like to add a generous pinch of salt to the sugar and butter so that the end result tastes almost like salted caramel, which pairs wonderfully with the apples and buttery dough.

# CAMPFIRE S'MORES BANANA BOATS

**12" SKILLET** / 5-Ingredient / One Pan / Quick & Easy / Vegetarian

**Serves 4 / Prep time: 5 minutes / Cook time: 10 minutes**

Talk about one of the easiest and most fun camping recipes. Kids especially love these banana boats, made right over the campfire in your trusty cast iron skillet. Marshmallows, chocolate, honey, and graham crackers get stuffed into a whole banana and charred over an open fire to gooey, melty bliss. Feel free to experiment with other toppings. Nuts, caramel sauce, peanut butter, coconut, butterscotch—the options are endless.

4 bananas

4 teaspoons honey

½ cup chopped milk chocolate or dark
   chocolate (or chocolate chips)

½ cup mini marshmallows

4 honey-flavored graham crackers

1. Preheat the skillet over the campfire until very hot.

2. Keep the entire peel on the bananas and split down the center lengthwise, without going all the way through.

3. Drizzle each banana boat with 1 teaspoon of honey, and fill each with 2 tablespoons of chocolate and 2 tablespoons of marshmallows. Crush a graham cracker over each banana.

4. Wrap the bananas in aluminum foil and lay them in the hot skillet. Cook until the chocolate and marshmallows are melted and the bananas are warmed through, about 10 minutes.

5. Carefully open foil packets and eat the banana boats with spoons.

**COOKING TIP:** Not a fan of camping? These banana boats can also be cooked in a 350°F oven or on the grill.

# PEAR CRUMBLE WITH GINGERBREAD STREUSEL

**12" SKILLET** / One Pan / Vegetarian / Weeknight

**Serves 6 / Prep time: 10 minutes / Cook time: 45 minutes**

During the winter and fall, you may suffer from apple overload. No offense, apples—you know I love you—but pears need attention, too. Pears are wonderful on their own, and delicious when baked into a warm, spiced crumble.

**FOR THE PEARS**

2 tablespoons unsalted butter

5 pears, peeled, cored, and cubed

¼ cup sugar

2 teaspoons grated fresh ginger

1 tablespoon all-purpose flour

1 teaspoon ground cinnamon

1 tablespoon molasses

1 tablespoon freshly squeezed
 lemon juice

**FOR THE CRUMBLE**

¾ cup rolled oats

¾ cup all-purpose flour

½ cup packed brown sugar

½ teaspoon salt

1½ teaspoons ground cinnamon

1 teaspoon ground ginger

¼ teaspoon ground nutmeg

¼ teaspoon ground cloves

6 tablespoons (¾ stick) unsalted
 butter, cubed

## TO MAKE THE PEARS

1. Preheat the oven to 375°F, and place the skillet over medium heat.

2. In the skillet, melt the butter. Add the diced pears, and sprinkle the sugar over top.

3. Cook the pears just until the sugar is dissolved. Stir in the ginger. Sprinkle the mixture with the flour and cinnamon. Cook for another minute, and stir in the molasses and lemon juice. Cook until bubbling.

## TO MAKE THE CRUMBLE

1. In a large bowl, whisk together the oats, flour, brown sugar, salt, cinnamon, ginger, nutmeg, and cloves. Using a pastry cutter or fork, cut the butter into the mixture until pea-size pieces remain and the streusel clumps when pinched.

2. Scatter the streusel evenly over the pears, and transfer to the oven. Bake until the topping is golden brown and the pears are bubbling and tender, 30 to 40 minutes.

# GRILLED PEACHES WITH HAZELNUTS AND WHIPPED HONEY MASCARPONE

**GRILL PAN** / Gluten-Free / Grain-Free / Quick & Easy / Vegetarian

**Serves 4 / Prep time: 10 minutes / Cook time: 10 minutes**

Nothing says summer like a ripe, juicy peach. When it comes to peaches at their peak, less is more. I like them best as close to their natural state as possible. Grilled peaches are an excellent way to bring out the sweetness of this fruit by caramelizing it. A cinnamon-scented honey butter helps glaze these sticky-sweet peaches, while whipped mascarpone imparts creaminess and hazelnuts add a pleasant crunch.

Extra-virgin olive oil, for greasing

2 tablespoons unsalted butter, melted

½ teaspoon ground cinnamon

4 tablespoons honey, divided, plus more for serving

2 ripe (but firm) peaches, halved and pitted

½ cup mascarpone

½ cup heavy (whipping) cream

½ teaspoon vanilla extract

½ teaspoon grated lemon zest

¼ cup chopped toasted hazelnuts

1. Preheat the grill pan over medium heat, and grease it lightly with olive oil.

2. In a small bowl, combine the melted butter with the cinnamon and 2 tablespoons of honey. Mix well and brush evenly over the peaches.

3. Place the peaches cut-side down on the hot grill. Cook until softened and caramelized with grill marks, 3 to 4 minutes. Flip over and continue cooking until the peaches are tender and heated through, about 4 minutes.

4. Meanwhile, make the whipped mascarpone. In a medium bowl, combine the remaining 2 tablespoons of honey with the mascarpone, heavy cream, vanilla, and lemon zest. Using a handheld mixer, beat the mixture until light and fluffy. Continue beating until stiff peaks form.

5. Serve each peach half with a dollop of the whipped mascarpone cream, and sprinkle with the chopped hazelnuts. Drizzle with additional honey, if desired.

**COOKING TIP:** This whipped honey mascarpone is also delicious with other dessert recipes, such as Greek Yogurt Apple Tarte Tatin (page 156) and Bourbon Baked Apples (page 166).

# GERMAN CHOCOLATE SKILLET COOKIE

**10" SKILLET, SMALL SAUCEPAN** / Vegetarian / Weeknight

**Serves 6 to 8 / Prep time: 25 minutes / Cook time: 20 minutes**

A traditional German chocolate cake topping crowns this nutty, chocolate-studded cookie.

## FOR THE COOKIE

Baking spray or unsalted butter,
  for greasing

8 tablespoons (1 stick) unsalted butter, at
  room temperature

½ cup packed brown sugar

½ cup white sugar

1 large egg

1 teaspoon vanilla extract

1 cup all-purpose flour

¼ cup cocoa powder

½ teaspoon baking soda

½ teaspoon salt

½ cup semisweet chocolate chips

½ cup toasted chopped pecans

## FOR THE TOPPING

¾ cup evaporated milk

¾ cup brown sugar

6 tablespoons (¾ stick) unsalted butter

2 large egg yolks

½ teaspoon vanilla extract

1 cup sweetened or unsweetened
  flaked coconut

¾ cup chopped pecans

¼ teaspoon salt

Pecan halves, for garnish (optional)

### TO MAKE THE COOKIE

1. Preheat the oven to 350°F, and grease the skillet with baking spray or butter.

2. In a large bowl, use a handheld electric mixer to cream the butter with the brown and white sugars until light and fluffy. Beat in the egg, then the vanilla.

3. In a medium bowl, sift together the flour, cocoa powder, baking soda, and salt. Beat the dry mixture into the butter mixture until just combined. Stir in the chocolate chips and pecans.

4. Spread the mixture evenly in the greased skillet.

5. Transfer to the oven and bake until the center is just set, about 20 minutes. Remove from the oven.

》》》

### TO MAKE THE TOPPING AND SERVE

1. Meanwhile, in a small saucepan over low heat, combine the evaporated milk, brown sugar, butter, and egg yolks. Cook, stirring constantly, until thick, 8 to 10 minutes. Remove from the heat and stir in the vanilla, coconut, pecans, and salt.

2. Transfer the mixture to a small bowl, cover, and refrigerate for at least 15 minutes to thicken. Remove the topping from the refrigerator when you take the cookie out of the oven. When the cookie has cooled to warm or room temperature, spoon on the topping and spread it out evenly.

3. Top the outer edge of the cookie with pecan halves, slice, and serve.

**STORAGE TIP:** The topping can be made 1 to 2 days in advance and stored in an airtight container in the refrigerator until ready to use. Let the topping come to room temperature before spreading.

# STRAWBERRIES AND CREAM SHORTCAKE SKILLET

**10" SKILLET** / One Pan / Vegetarian / Weeknight

Serves 6 / Prep time: 15 minutes / Cook time: 35 minutes

This skillet is basically a deconstructed, one-pan shortcake. Honeyed strawberries are crowned with a shortcake crumble topping and baked in the oven until golden and bubbly. Be sure to serve this skillet warm with plenty of lightly sweetened whipped cream.

## FOR THE STRAWBERRIES

Unsalted butter, for greasing

2 pounds strawberries, hulled and quartered

2 tablespoons freshly squeezed lemon juice

1 tablespoon cornstarch

½ cup sugar

¼ cup honey

## FOR THE TOPPING

1½ cups all-purpose flour

2 tablespoons baking powder

¼ teaspoon salt

2 tablespoons sugar

4 tablespoons cold unsalted butter, cubed

½ cup heavy (whipping) cream

### TO MAKE THE STRAWBERRIES

1. Preheat the oven to 375°F, and grease the skillet with butter.

2. In a large bowl, toss together the strawberries, lemon juice, cornstarch, sugar, and honey. Transfer to the skillet.

### TO MAKE THE TOPPING AND SERVE

1. In a large bowl, combine the flour, baking powder, salt, and sugar. Using a pastry cutter or fork, cut the butter into the flour until it is broken up into pea-size pieces. Pour in the cream, and mix until just combined.

2. Spoon mounds of the topping mixture over the strawberries in the skillet, and flatten each mound slightly with your hand.

3. Transfer to the oven, bake until golden brown, 30 to 35 minutes, and serve.

# FIVE-SPICE BANANA CHEESECAKE EGG ROLLS

**12″ SKILLET** / One Pan / Quick & Easy / Vegetarian

Serves 6 / Prep time: 15 minutes / Cook time: 5 minutes

This recipe is inspired by a dessert we created when I worked on the pastry team for the Manchester Grand Hyatt in San Diego. The unique addition is the Chinese five-spice powder, a mix of sweet and spicy cinnamon, fennel, clove, star anise, and black pepper. It adds a fragrant and warm heat, but you could always swap it for cinnamon if you'd prefer.

Vegetable oil, for frying

1 (8-ounce) block whole-fat cream cheese, at room temperature

¼ cup whole-fat sour cream

1 teaspoon vanilla extract

¾ teaspoon Chinese five-spice powder

½ cup confectioners' sugar

Pinch salt

6 egg roll wrappers

2 bananas, peeled

Honey, for drizzling

1. Preheat the skillet over medium heat with 2 inches of vegetable oil.

2. In a medium bowl, combine the cream cheese, sour cream, vanilla, five-spice powder, sugar, and salt. Beat until combined.

3. Lay an egg roll wrapper on a clean surface in the shape of a diamond with one point facing you. Spoon 2 heaping tablespoons of the cream cheese in a line down the center of the wrapper.

4. Cut each banana into 3 pieces. Top the cream cheese with a banana piece. Tightly roll up the bottom half of the egg roll. Tuck in the sides and brush the open end with water. Roll and seal the egg roll. Repeat with the remaining egg rolls, cream cheese mixture, and banana pieces.

5. Fry the egg rolls in the hot oil until browned, 2 to 3 minutes per side.

6. Transfer to a paper towel–lined plate to drain and cool. Serve drizzled with honey.

**COOKING TIP:** You can make the cream cheese mixture the day before, and I recommend doing so. A cold filling is less likely to leak out during frying.

# BLACKBERRY-LAVENDER COBBLER

**10" SKILLET** / One Pan / Vegetarian / Weeknight

**Serves 6 / Prep time: 15 minutes / Cook time: 45 minutes**

I love lavender in anything, but it pairs especially well with blackberries to make this light, summery cobbler. A buttermilk batter is the perfect match for this floral, berry-studded dish.

Baking spray or unsalted butter, for
  greasing
1 tablespoon dried culinary lavender
1¼ cups sugar
12 ounces fresh ripe blackberries
1 tablespoon freshly squeezed
  lemon juice

1 cup all-purpose flour
1 tablespoon baking powder
¼ teaspoon salt
4 tablespoons (½ stick) unsalted
  butter, melted
1 cup buttermilk

1. Preheat the oven to 375°F, and grease the skillet with baking spray or butter.

2. Place the lavender in the bowl of a food processor and pulse until it is broken up into small pieces. Add the sugar and continue pulsing until the lavender is finely chopped and evenly incorporated into the sugar.

3. In a medium bowl, combine ¼ cup of lavender sugar with the blackberries and lemon juice.

4. In a large bowl, whisk together the flour, ¾ cup of lavender sugar, and the baking powder and salt. Whisk in the melted butter and buttermilk until combined.

5. Pour the batter into the greased skillet. Scatter the blackberries evenly over the batter. (The blackberries will sink to the bottom while baking.)

6. Sprinkle the top evenly with the remaining 2 tablespoons of lavender sugar. Transfer the cobbler to the oven and bake until golden brown, about 45 minutes. Remove from the oven and let cool slightly before slicing and serving.

**VARIATION TIP:** You can swap out the blackberries in this cobbler for blueberries, which also pair nicely with lavender.

# BOURBON BAKED APPLES

**10" SKILLET** / One Pan / Vegetarian / Weeknight

Serves 6 / Prep time: 10 minutes / Cook time: 45 minutes

I adore these baked apples, filled with a buttery, nutty streusel and scented with cinnamon and vanilla. The apples sit atop a pool of bourbon and sparkling apple cider, which reduces in the oven into a boozy caramel.

6 baking apples, such as Honeycrisp,
  Pink Lady, or Gala

½ cup rolled oats

½ cup packed brown sugar

2 tablespoons all-purpose flour

3 tablespoons chopped walnuts

1 teaspoon ground cinnamon

½ teaspoon salt

1 teaspoon vanilla extract

4 tablespoons (½ stick) unsalted
  butter, cubed

½ cup sparkling apple cider, such
  as Martinelli's

½ cup bourbon

Vanilla ice cream, for serving

1. Preheat the oven to 400°F.

2. Wash the apples, but do not peel them. Using an apple corer, cut out the center and all of the seeds, but do not go all the way through to the bottom.

3. In a medium bowl, mix together the oats, brown sugar, flour, walnuts, cinnamon, salt, and vanilla. Using your fingers, a fork, or a pastry cutter, cut the butter into the dry mixture until it is broken down into pea-size pieces. The streusel should clump together when pinched.

4. Arrange the apples upright in the skillet. Evenly fill each apple center with the streusel mixture, packing it down as compact as possible. Pack small mounds of the streusel on top of each apple.

5. In a small bowl, whisk the sparkling cider and bourbon together. Pour into the pan.

6. Loosely cover the pan with aluminum foil and transfer to the oven. Bake, covered, for 25 minutes.

7. Remove the foil at the 25-minute mark, and continue baking, uncovered, until the apples are tender, the filling is golden brown, and the sauce has bubbled and reduced down, about 20 more minutes.

8. Carefully remove from the oven and let cool for 5 minutes. Serve the apples with vanilla ice cream, and drizzle with the sauce from the skillet.

# COCONUT OIL SKILLET BROWNIE

**10" SKILLET** / One Pan / Vegetarian / Weeknight

**Serves 8 / Prep time: 15 minutes / Cook time: 25 minutes**

If you're a fan of coconut oil, these brownies are a must. This skillet brownie is rich, decadent, and very fudgy—perfect both spooned warm from the pan with ice cream or cut into wedges. These brownies can also accommodate dairy-free diets, and they taste just as amazing the next day.

Unsalted butter or baking spray, for greasing

½ cup coconut oil, measured in liquid state

5 ounces semisweet or dark chocolate, chopped

½ cup white sugar

½ cup packed brown sugar

2 large eggs, beaten

1 teaspoon vanilla extract

½ cup all-purpose flour

½ teaspoon salt

2 tablespoons cocoa powder

Ice cream, for serving (optional)

1.  Preheat the oven to 350°F, and grease the skillet very well with butter or baking spray.

2.  Using a water bath or a medium-size microwavable bowl in the microwave, slowly melt the coconut oil and chocolate until smooth, stirring frequently.

3.  Whisk in the white and brown sugars until smooth. Whisk in the eggs and vanilla.

4.  Sift together the flour, salt, and cocoa powder, and fold into the batter until completely incorporated, being careful not to overmix.

5.  Pour the batter into the skillet, and transfer to the oven. Bake until the edges are set and a toothpick inserted into the center comes out mostly clean with a few crumbs, about 25 minutes. This will result in a fudgy brownie.

6.  Let the brownie cool for 5 minutes and serve warm with ice cream (if desired), or let it cool completely and cut into 8 to 10 wedges.

**COOKING TIP:** You could also make this recipe using 4 individual brownie skillets. Bake in 3½-inch mini cast iron pans, and serve each topped with ice cream.

# PEANUT BUTTER AND JELLY SKILLET COOKIE

**10" SKILLET** / One Pan / Vegetarian / Weeknight

**Serves 6 to 8 / Prep time: 10 minutes / Cook time: 25 minutes**

Skillet cookie, meet PB&J. This dessert combines classic childhood favorites: creamy peanut butter, peanut butter chips, and a fruity jam center. Little ones love this skillet, and best of all, it's easy to whip up. Serve warm with vanilla ice cream for an extra treat.

Baking spray or butter, for greasing

8 tablespoons (1 stick) unsalted butter, at room temperature

½ cup packed brown sugar

⅓ cup white sugar

½ cup creamy peanut butter

1 large egg

1 teaspoon vanilla extract

1⅓ cups all-purpose flour

½ teaspoon baking soda

½ teaspoon salt

½ cup peanut butter chips

½ cup jam (see tip), divided

1. Preheat the oven to 350°F, and grease the skillet liberally with baking spray or butter.

2. In the bowl of a standing mixer or in a large bowl using a handheld electric mixer, beat the butter with both sugars until light and fluffy. Beat in the peanut butter, then the egg and vanilla.

3. In a medium bowl, whisk the flour, baking soda, and salt together; add to the butter mixture in two additions. Mix until just combined, but do not overmix.

4. Fold in the peanut butter chips.

5. Spread half of the batter in the bottom of the cast iron pan. Spoon on all but 2 tablespoons of jam; spread it out evenly. Spread the other half of the peanut butter batter on top, and place the skillet in the oven.

6. Bake until the cookie is golden and set but the center is still soft (it will firm as it cools), about 25 minutes. Remove from the oven and let cool slightly.

7. Warm the remaining 2 tablespoons of jam in a microwavable mug in the microwave. Drizzle the jam over the cookie and serve.

**COOKING TIP:** The type of jam is up to you. Keep it basic with strawberry or grape, or mix things up with a blueberry-lemon or tart cherry. To make the jam easier to spread in the center of the cookie, warm it a little in the microwave.

# FRIED CANNOLI CRISPS WITH RUM-RICOTTA DIP

**12" SKILLET** / One Pan / Vegetarian / Weeknight

**Serves 8 / Prep time: 25 minutes / Cook time: 15 minutes**

If you've ever seen *The Godfather*, you know the famous quote, "Leave the gun; take the cannoli." This recipe is kind of like "Leave the cannoli; take the flavor profile." This deconstructed cannoli features a rummy, orange-scented cream and golden dough crisps. All the flavor of traditional cannoli, with a lot less work.

## FOR THE CANNOLI CRISPS

3 cups all-purpose flour, plus more
   for dusting

¼ cup sugar, plus more for sprinkling

1 teaspoon ground cinnamon, plus more
   for sprinkling

½ teaspoon salt

6 tablespoons (¾ stick) unsalted butter

1 large egg

1 large egg yolk

½ cup Marsala wine

Vegetable oil, for frying

## FOR THE DIP

1 cup whole-milk ricotta cheese

8 ounces mascarpone cheese

Pinch salt

1 cup confectioners' sugar

1 teaspoon vanilla extract

¼ teaspoon ground cinnamon

¼ teaspoon grated orange zest

2 tablespoons rum

1 cup finely chopped semisweet
   chocolate

Chopped toasted pistachios, for garnish
   (optional)

### TO MAKE THE CANNOLI CRISPS

1.  Preheat the skillet over medium heat.

2.  In a large bowl, whisk together the flour, sugar, cinnamon, and salt. Using a pastry cutter or fork, cut the butter into the flour until it is broken up into pea-size pieces.

3. Make a well in the center of the mixture, and add the egg, egg yolk, and Marsala. Stir to combine. Pour the mixture onto a lightly floured surface and knead for 5 minutes by hand, until a smooth dough forms.

4. Divide into 2 discs, wrap with plastic wrap, and let sit in the refrigerator for at least 10 minutes while you make the dip.

5. Add 2 inches of vegetable oil to the bottom of the pan. Heat the oil to 350°F.

6. Chill the discs and make the dip.

7. Using your hands or a pasta machine, roll out each half of the cannoli until paper-thin.

8. Using a circle cutter, cut the cannoli dough into rounds. Alternatively, use a pizza cutter to make triangles.

9. Fry the cannoli crisps in the hot oil in batches until golden, 1 to 2 minutes per side. Drain on a paper towel–lined plate and repeat until all crisps are fried. Sprinkle with cinnamon sugar while still hot, if desired, and serve with the dip.

### TO MAKE THE DIP

1. In a large bowl, use a handheld mixer to beat the ricotta and mascarpone until combined. Add the salt and confectioners' sugar, and continue beating until light and fluffy.

2. Beat in the vanilla, cinnamon, orange zest, and rum. Fold in the chocolate. Garnish with chopped pistachios, if desired.

**COOKING TIP:** To save time, skip the homemade dough and fry halved wonton wrappers instead. Sprinkle them with cinnamon sugar after frying.

# SKILLET THREE-NUT BAKLAVA PIE

**12" SKILLET** / One Pan / Vegetarian / Weeknight

Serves 8 / Prep time: 15 minutes / Cook time: 35 minutes

My husband despises nuts in desserts, so much so that he used to have his mom pick out the nuts, one by one, from his butter pecan ice cream. Now that's something only a mother would do. When I made this recipe, I didn't think he'd even try it. He took the tiniest bite of mine . . . then ate two big slices. This pie is inspired by baklava, as pecans, walnuts, and pistachios combine with a honeyed filling and a phyllo crust.

Baking spray or unsalted butter,
  for greasing

10 sheets frozen phyllo dough, thawed

12 tablespoons (1½ sticks) unsalted
  butter, divided

½ cup packed brown sugar, divided

½ cup white sugar, divided

1 tablespoon ground cinnamon

¾ cup honey

1 teaspoon vanilla extract

¾ teaspoon salt

2 tablespoons bourbon

1 teaspoon grated orange zest

3 large eggs

¾ cup chopped toasted walnuts

1 cup chopped toasted pecans

½ cup chopped toasted pistachios

1.  Preheat the oven to 375°F, and grease the skillet very well with baking spray or butter.

2.  Unwrap the phyllo sheets one by one. Melt 1 stick of butter. In a small bowl, combine ¼ cup of brown sugar, ¼ cup of white sugar, and the cinnamon. Brush both sides of a phyllo sheet with butter, and sprinkle on a tablespoon of the cinnamon-sugar mixture. Do the same with another phyllo sheet, and place it on top. Place the double phyllo sheet in the skillet.

3.  Repeat this process with the remaining phyllo sheets, arranging them in the skillet to cover the bottom and sides and form the crust. Brush the hanging edges with melted butter.

4. In a medium microwave-safe bowl, melt the remaining ¼ cup of butter. Whisk in the remaining ¼ cup each of brown and white sugars, along with the honey, vanilla, salt, bourbon, and orange zest.

5. Whisk in the eggs, one at a time, until combined.

6. Lay all of the nuts in the prepared skillet on top of the phyllo dough. Pour in the honey custard. Gently fold the hanging edges of the phyllo over the top of the pie.

7. Bake until the center is set and the crust is golden, about 35 minutes. Let cool completely before slicing and serving.

***VARIATION TIP:*** Use any combination of nuts here that you'd like.

# LEMON AND MINT OLIVE OIL SKILLET CAKE

**12" SKILLET, SMALL SAUCEPAN** / Vegetarian / Weeknight

Serves 8 / Prep time: 15 minutes / Cook time: 25 minutes

This Italian-inspired cake combines fruity extra-virgin olive oil with fresh mint and a tart lemon syrup. The syrup ensures that the cake is moist but not too sweet. Serve this cake in the summer topped with whipped cream.

**FOR THE CAKE**

Unsalted butter or baking spray, for greasing

½ cup extra-virgin olive oil

1 cup sugar

3 large eggs

1 tablespoon grated lemon zest

2 tablespoons chopped fresh mint

1⅓ cups all-purpose flour

½ teaspoon baking soda

1 teaspoon baking powder

¼ teaspoon salt

⅓ cup whole milk

**FOR THE SYRUP**

½ cup sugar

½ cup water

1 tablespoon lemon zest

¼ cup freshly squeezed lemon juice

⅓ cup fresh mint leaves, torn

**FOR SERVING**

Whipped cream (optional)

Fresh berries (optional)

## TO MAKE THE CAKE

1. Preheat the oven to 350°F, and grease the skillet very well with butter or baking spray.

2. In a large bowl, whisk together the olive oil and sugar. Beat in the eggs, one at a time, followed by the lemon zest and mint.

3. In a medium bowl, whisk together the flour, baking soda, baking powder, and salt.

4. Whisk the flour mixture into the olive oil mixture, alternating with the milk.

5. Whisk the cake batter until smooth, but do not overmix.

6. Pour the cake batter into the prepared skillet, transfer to the oven, and bake until the top is golden and a tester comes out clean, about 25 minutes.

### TO MAKE THE SYRUP

1. Meanwhile, in a small saucepan, bring the sugar, water, lemon zest, lemon juice, and mint to a boil. Remove from the heat and let infuse for 20 minutes, then strain.

2. After the cake has been out of the oven for 15 minutes, use a skewer to poke holes all over it. Evenly brush on the lemon-mint syrup.

3. Serve with whipped cream and fresh berries, if desired.

**VARIATION TIP:** Instead of mint, try using fresh basil; it also pairs well with lemon and is lovely in desserts. I like this cake with whipped cream and fresh berries, but it's delicious on its own.

# BROWN BUTTER PINEAPPLE UPSIDE-DOWN CAKE

**10" SKILLET** / One Pan / Vegetarian

**Serves 6 / Prep time: 15 minutes / Cook time: 45 minutes, plus 10 minutes to cool**

I grew up accustomed to the canned pineapple upside-down cakes with a maraschino cherry in each ring's center. This classic cake was made popular in the 1920s, when the Hawaiian Pineapple Company ran a recipe contest and had a flood of pineapple upside-down cake submissions. However, upside-down cakes of all varieties were being baked in cast iron skillets as far back as the 1800s. This grown-up spin on the classic combines brown butter with sweet, caramelized pineapple.

12 tablespoons (1 ½ sticks) unsalted butter, divided

½ cup packed brown sugar

1 cup sliced fresh pineapple

¾ cup white sugar

1 teaspoon vanilla extract

2 large eggs

1½ cups all-purpose flour

1 teaspoon baking powder

½ teaspoon baking soda

¼ teaspoon salt

½ cup buttermilk

¼ cup pineapple juice

1. Preheat the oven to 350°F, and preheat the skillet over medium heat.

2. In the skillet, cook 1 stick of the butter until it is nutty, brown, and fragrant, about 6 minutes. Stir the butter often, keeping a close eye to ensure that it does not burn.

3. Pour the butter into a shallow dish and place it in the freezer to stiffen for 10 to 15 minutes.

4. Meanwhile, melt the remaining ½ stick of butter in the skillet, and sprinkle on the brown sugar. Cook just until the sugar is dissolved and the butter is bubbling, then remove from the heat.

5. Lay the sliced pineapple on top of the caramel in the skillet in a nice pattern.

6. Once the browned butter is cold and solid, place it in a large bowl and use a hand mixer to cream it with the white sugar until fluffy. Beat in the vanilla and eggs.

7. In a medium bowl, whisk together the flour, baking powder, baking soda, and salt.

8. Beat the flour mixture into the egg mixture, alternating with the buttermilk and pineapple juice, until just combined.

9. Pour the batter on top of the pineapple, and transfer to the oven. Bake until the cake is golden and a tester inserted into the center comes out clean, 30 to 40 minutes.

10. Let the cake cool for 10 minutes before inverting onto a large plate, slicing, and serving.

**VARIATION TIP:** Once you master the basics of upside-down cake, experiment with different fruits. Rhubarb, pears, berries, peaches, and figs are all delicious.

# measurement conversions

| US STANDARD | US STANDARD (OUNCES) | METRIC (APPROXIMATE) |
| --- | --- | --- |
| 2 tablespoons | 1 fl. oz. | 30 mL |
| ¼ cup | 2 fl. oz. | 60 mL |
| ½ cup | 4 fl. oz. | 120 mL |
| 1 cup | 8 fl. oz. | 240 mL |
| 1½ cups | 12 fl. oz. | 355 mL |
| 2 cups or 1 pint | 16 fl. oz. | 475 mL |
| 4 cups or 1 quart | 32 fl. oz. | 1 L |
| 1 gallon | 128 fl. oz. | 4 L |

| FAHRENHEIT (F) | CELSIUS (C) (APPROXIMATE) |
| --- | --- |
| 250°F | 120°C |
| 300°F | 150°C |
| 325°F | 165°C |
| 350°F | 180°C |
| 375°F | 190°C |
| 400°F | 200°C |
| 425°F | 220°C |
| 450°F | 230°C |

## VOLUME EQUIVALENTS (DRY)

| US STANDARD | METRIC (APPROXIMATE) |
| --- | --- |
| ¼ teaspoon | 1 mL |
| ½ teaspoon | 2 mL |
| 1 teaspoon | 5 mL |
| 1 tablespoon | 15 mL |
| ¼ cup | 59 mL |
| ⅓ cup | 79 mL |
| ½ cup | 118 mL |
| 1 cup | 177 mL |
| 2 cups or 1 pint | 475 mL |
| 3 cups | 700 mL |
| 4 cups or 1 quart | 1 L |

## WEIGHT EQUIVALENTS

| US STANDARD | METRIC (APPROXIMATE) |
| --- | --- |
| ½ ounce | 15 g |
| 1 ounce | 30 g |
| 2 ounces | 60 g |
| 4 ounces | 115 g |
| 8 ounces | 225 g |
| 12 ounces | 340 g |
| 16 ounces or 1 pound | 455 g |

# index

# Acknowledgments

To my husband, Ryan—thank you for always supporting me, making me laugh, and doing the dishes. (I know there were a lot of them during the creation of this cookbook.) You are my favorite person and my foundation, and I love exploring this world by your side.

To my mom—my Josie and my best friend, thank you for always being my biggest fan and encouraging me to follow my dreams. You always give me the strength I need (literally, too—you make a mean cup of coffee) and believe in me when I do not believe in myself. You are the kindest heart I have ever known.

To my dad—thank you, Pop, for serving our country and showing me that bravery is not about being fearless, but doing something great in spite of that fear. Thank you for teaching me the importance of hard work, resilience, and a sense of humor when everything goes wrong.

To those who helped make this cookbook possible, or even a little easier—thank you a million times over. Thank you to Sara Grohsman for being my longest friend and one of the best chefs I know, and for helping me recipe test, even during (and on) the holidays. Thank you to Tish Pacheco for being one of my favorite humans, keeping me sane, and always making me laugh. Thank you to Angela, Uncle Joe, Grandma, Sheila, Bill, and the rest of my family for always supporting me through thick and thin (and letting me tease you a bit in this book). Thank you to Shannon Graham for being an amazing assistant and helping me research and recipe test. Thank you to Tricia Bozeman for being my favorite blogger and giving me a hand with recipe testing. And thank you to Sam Nasserian and my colleagues at Cozymeal for your patience and support. To "The Outsiders," thank you for making Monday nights so much fun!

To the readers of *Parsnips and Pastries*, new or old—thank you, from the bottom of my heart, for your continued support.

To Clara Song Lee, Vanessa Putt, Myryah Irby, and the rest of the Callisto Media team—thank you for being incredible to work with and for trusting me, inspiring me, and allowing me to share my passion for cast iron cooking.

*CIN-CIN!*

# *About the Author*

**Tiffany La Forge** is a professional chef, recipe developer, and food writer who runs the blog *Parsnips and Pastries.* Her blog centers on her passion—creating seasonal, balanced, and approachable recipes and meals meant to be shared with others.

Tiffany graduated from the Institute of Culinary Education in New York City and has worked at Michelin-star restaurants, bakeries, and hotels throughout the country. Her writing and recipes have been featured at James Beard Taste America as well as in publications like *Prevention* and *Elle* and on websites like Healthline, Yahoo Lifestyle, MSN, and Brit + Co.

She lives with her husband and corgi in the Pacific Northwest. When she's not in the kitchen, Tiffany enjoys yoga, traveling, champagne, gardening, and copious amounts of coffee. Learn more and explore free recipes at www.ParsnipsandPastries.com.

www.ingramcontent.com/pod-product-compliance
Lightning Source LLC
Chambersburg PA
CBHW060945100426
42813CB00016B/2864